A CRAFTY CIGARETTE

Tales of a Teenager Mod
as Seen through His Eyes

Matteo Sedazzari

Disclaimer by the author on *Crafty Cigarette*.

In order to give the novel a realistic feel, it was my intention to keep the narrative simple, complete with deliberate grammatical errors. I wanted to present an authentic account in the first person by the lead character who is only 11 years of age at the beginning of the story. Therefore, understandably, his command of the English language is simple and he will at times make errors, as he is still a child, and not an educated adult reminiscing in acute detail in an articulate and eloquent manner.

Thank you for buying the book

www.zani.co.uk

Crafty Cigarette is dedicated to Patricia Rochester (Sedazzari), my mother, for being there at the very start of my life (stating the bleeding obvious) x and to Jimmy AKA James Constantinou, Richard Knights & Tim Bryan… thank you for making my life as a teenager mad, fun and beautiful, it was a laugh! Didn't we have a nice time!!! Special thanks to Alan McGee for the sage advice over the years. John Cooper Clarke for the inspiration.. Paul McEvoy for the vision and support. Cathal Smyth AKA Chas Smash of Madness, for laughing out loud at my jokes. Loren Jenkins for the coffees and chats. Nick Taylor, for being a true prince amongst gentleman. Tracey Dawn Wilmot for the giggles. Laurence Parmiter, a true friend and top fighter. Simon Bell, for being a top fella. Chris Madden, for always listening. Dean Cavanagh for the in-depth chats over the years. Simon Wells for sharing his wisdom with me. Julia Mottram for the friendship and love. Mahen Kara for always uplifting my soul. Adam Bishop, Tim Mardell, Dave Powell, Kevin Barry and Paul McEvoy (again!) from Friends Of Luca Brasi for rocking the Spice of Life time and again. Paolo Sedazzari for introducing me to so much. Ian Page and David Cairns of Secret Affair, for giving me a more in-depth meaning to Mod. Dave Barlow, a top bloke and a great web designer. Paul Weller, Rick Buckler and Bruce Foxton AKA The Jam for giving me so much drive at such at an early age, you really are the best fxxking band in the world! All the boys and girls with Mod sensibilities across the world. All the pretty PA's plotting revenge against their bosses, and finally Juventus & the Italian national football team, for giving me so much joy … and tears.

Love, Peace and Chaos

Matteo Sedazzari
Sept 2015
X

Foreword by John Cooper Clarke

Anybody who is anybody has worn the three button uniform and that's official. Mod is a train of thought and its destination is the personal refinement and ultimate sophistication of the individual citizen by way of his own aesthetic judgement. The production values of Mod persist even into old age (unless some kind of severe mental breakdown intervenes) because their agility is non restrictive. The Neapolitan or Continental suit for example, was popularised in America and given to the World in movies, why, because it is class, classless and looks good on all shapes. Matteo Sedazzari got the Modinest bug from the sharp silhouettes of his heroes, Rick Buckler, Bruce Foxton and Paul Weller AKA The Jam and who could deny their monochrome allure. It's almost impossible to write the way you speak (name one) but Signor Sedazzari has that gift, and in his chuckle heavy account of his teenage escapades, obsessions, senseless capers of one kind or another, and his good humoured keeping of the faith in the face of disappointment, has film treatment written all over it. I even get a name check but rest assured no gratuitous ego massage took place in this transaction. From time to time he is apologetic and accuses himself of boring you with the details, but this is our world today where the details are in the field and dressed by such a discerning eye, magical. I couldn't put it down because I couldn't put it down.

John Cooper Clarke August 2015

Contents

I

1977 – The Angry Mob of Sunbury

"You bastards" brutal words that wake me from my beauty sleep. I'm not alarmed, just wondering why it's taken him so long. Again I hear more screams followed by more swear words, and then the sound of the bedside lamps in my parents and brother's rooms being switched on, with sleepy murmurs. I am laughing inside, serves the bastard right, always telling me off, telling my parents what I have done. Not that they listen, they despise him as much as I do. I pull my curtain back, but I don't switch any lights on, I think I saw this in an American cop show or Colditz. Leave the light off, then you can see better and your enemy can't see you. As I gaze out, many of the neighbours from the houses opposite and next to ours are coming out to see what the commotion is about. Whilst their children, many I go to school with, look out from their windows or stand by the front door in fear. It's a wonderful sight that warms my heart.

Tomorrow's going to be a huge street party for all of us, just like there will be across all of Great Britain, as it's the Queen's Silver Jubilee. 25 years I think she's been Queen. I don't really understand what she does, apart from living in a palace in London and having a castle in Windsor. I like the Safari Park there and, oh yes, she does a speech on Christmas Day at 3 o'clock, which my father always turns off. Yet everyone is excited, adults and children alike.

Me, looking forward to the party, sausage rolls, chips, cakes and sweets followed by games with my "friends". I put friends in inverted commas as we are not close, just a level of acceptance and toleration due to the fact our parents are friends, we live in the same close, Ravendale Road and most of us attended the same school, Nursery Road Middle School, Sunbury, Middlesex. Yet I am the outsider, due to my heritage, I have an Italian father, so for many years I have been ridiculed not just by my class mates but the bloody teachers as well. "Italians were cowards in the Second World War, an Italian tank with 1 gear going forward and 13 reverse gears going back. The Italian Book of Heroes, with only one page." This was every day, not so much now. Been to Italy quite a few times for the family holiday, (most of the kids in my school go to Butlin's or Bognor Regis), love Italy and the food. My father works in Covent Garden market and brings back genuine Italian food from Soho, much better than any school dinner I've ever tasted.

The teasing is more about football now, how England won the World Cup just over ten years ago, and the last time Italy won it was before the Second World War. But last year I got my revenge when Italy beat England two nil with goals from Giancarlo Antognoni and Roberto Bettega, an important game, could get us into the World Cup. The kids said they will get revenge when they play us later this year at Wembley, but my older brother tells me we have a better goal difference and look good to qualify. Seen the goals twice on the BBC, blink and you will miss it, but in my head I relive Bettega's header over and over again. It's my imagination that helps me to escape the boredom of the playground and the classroom. I read Batman and Spiderman comics, watch Horror films, Hammer or Universal. I'm lucky as my parents let me stay up late to watch ITV's Appointment of Fear on a Monday night, which is usually a Hammer Horror film and the Horror double bill on a Saturday night, which was usually a Universal followed by a Hammer film. How Christopher Lee and Bela Lugosi scare me, how I cheer for Peter Cushing, and how I tingle when Barbara Shelley or Ingrid Pitt comes on the screen. I go to bed dreaming of fighting vampires, rescuing beautiful women and scoring a goal for Italy, just like Bettega.

I suppose I started speaking to class mates more when I became interested in football. My brother loves football, always reading up on it. He's 'football crazy' as they say. At the start of this year, I watched Juventus play for the first time against Manchester United in the UEFA Cup, highlights on Sportsnight. Juventus lost but before a tear could run down my cheek, my brother said don't worry they will beat them in Turin. Then he explained about the two legs and told me all about the team like their great goalkeeper Dino Zoff and how most of the team play for Italy. My brother was right, Juventus beat Manchester United 3 nil two weeks later, yet for some strange reason they didn't show the highlights on Sportsnight. Found out by listening to the radio, went to sleep very happy. I watched Italy in the 1974 World Cup but after they went out my interest in football dwindled, but since Italy beat England and seeing Juventus, I've become 'football crazy' like my brother. We play Subbuteo all the time, my skills have got better, and lately I have played round some of the other kid's houses. I got a football sticker album at the start of the year, became interested in England's Division One, talk to some of the boys now about football, as none of them like Batman or Dracula.

Not really keen on music, my parents or my brother don't buy records, and the only time I listen to music is at my grandparents in Essex. Like some of their music, The Beatles' a Red and Blue LP, but I don't like the bands on Top of the Pops, find them stupid. A lot of the girls at school sing a load of the songs, like Tiger Feet or something, and dance together, but I like The Monkees, they have a TV show, it's on the BBC. Four men who get up to all sorts of adventures, my brother tells me they are from America and split up a long time ago, as have the Beatles. However this year, everyone is talking about punk, I have never heard a punk song, but there's this band called The Sex Pistols who have made a record called God Save The Queen, it's having a go at the Queen, it's been banned, never knew music could be so dangerous, I like naughty things oh yes. My teacher, Mrs Roberts, told us about punk parties, where they make you drink urine, eat cakes filled with drugs, and after you've eaten them, you are a drug addict, just like the ones you see on the TV cop show, Kojak, I like Kojak as well. I ask her, all innocently, if she had been to a punk party, most of the class were in shock, there were a few sniggers and I was sent to the headmistress, but I wasn't joking, I was just wondering how she knew so much. My father always told me to question everything; especially if it's a doctor, a policeman or a teacher.

The other day Mickey Davies, one of the 'rough kids', was holding court in the playground, like he often does. Mickey is alright with me; anyway he's telling us that his older brother, Bob, is a punk and had seen The Sex Pistols. I was about to ask whether he had drunk any piss, but Mickey is tougher than me, so I thought best not.

Opposite and two doors down from me, lives a teenager called Peter with his parents. He has never spoken to me, just glares at me when I am outside kicking a ball against the wall or up the tree in the garden looking out. He has a girlfriend, both are starting to dress punk, only seen it on the TV or photos in my father's Sunday Times, but from the photos I have seen and how they dress, I am safe in saying they are punks. Peter and his girlfriend suddenly became the talk of the close, well it's not a close, there's a road going through it with a nice block of houses in the middle. I often go shopping with my mother and she bumps into neighbours in Key Markets, the green grocers, the newsagent, and how they would tell my mother it's a disgrace the way Peter and his girlfriend dress and how they must be on drugs. My mother never puts the knife in, just nods in agreement. I find it odd, that someone could be so hated for the way they dress.

Yesterday I was watching some of the neighbours, including my mother, putting up tables, hanging Union Jacks from the lamp posts, and lots of photographs of the Queen. My father was too busy having a snooze and my brother was reading World Soccer, and I was happy watching them work. Then I had an idea, which was followed by uncontrollable laughter, just like The Joker from Batman, which woke my father up and he shouted out for me to shut up.

I waited until the sun went down and decided to go in the back garden to kick a ball around, my parents are happy for me to do this, and I am not really sent to bed early. On the way to the garden, I went into my brother's room and stole a black marker pen. Like Batman, I managed to open the gate that is at the side of the house without making a sound. I walked into where everything was set for tomorrow's party, and I started to draw moustaches on the photos of the Queen, well the ones I could reach anyway. I kept looking round, hoping no one would be looking out of their window. Must have taken five minutes before I crept back into the garden, quietly closing the gate behind me. I went back into the house to watch some TV with the rest of my family. I was thrilled and delighted, knowing full well this would send Mr Bates, the party organiser, insane. For months he's been chatting about the Queen and The Jubilee, like she's his aunt or something. My brother reckons he plays the National Anthem before he goes to bed and wears a Union Jack waistcoat, like Tim Brooke Taylor from The Goodies. The image makes me chuckle.

I thought Mr Bates or someone would see my work of art before I went to bed. But it had just gone one in the morning before he did. I knew he would go out for one last inspection before the great day, and yes, there he is, before my eyes going ape. No one, not even his wife goes near him, then he points at Peter's house, "It's that fucking Peter and his whore of a girlfriend", I have never heard him use the f word before, he starts marching towards the house, followed by some of the neighbours, just like the villagers coming together to burn down Frankenstein's castle. The laughter has gone, I didn't expect this, I was beginning to like Peter, he was different and my brother had started talking to him

Peter's father, who hadn't come out beforehand, I think he's like my parents he can't stand Mr Bates, opens the front door as he must have heard the advancing angry mob. From my window I could

5

see Peter's father followed by his mother, he doesn't seem to fear Mr Bates and the 'villagers'. Peter's father just put his hands forward to gesture for him to stop but Mr Bates throws one punch and Peter's father is knocked down. Peter's mother goes to his aid and the women of the group pull her back, but she is putting up a good fight. As she is doing this, Mr Bates marches straight into the house followed by the men of the group. I am hoping that Peter and his girlfriend are out, but my wishes aren't granted, as this horde of men are dragging Peter and his girlfriend out. Peter is trying to fight them off as is his girlfriend, but the mob is too strong for them. Both in their night wear, and his girlfriend is very curvy, but this isn't the time to fancy a girl. I can't move, my mouth is dry and I'm unable to speak. The mob is holding the teenagers, who are wriggling like eels trying to get away. Mr Bates walks off to his house, what is he going to get - a cane? No he comes back with a rope, a bloody rope he's going to hang them. This is madness and it's all my fault. Mr Bates throws the rope over the lamp post, just like the cowboys do in those western films, am I about to witness a murder? No one is trying to stop him, and even the angry mob are still gripping the teenagers, so what if Peter and his girl don't like the Queen, well in fact they might do, because it was me that drew the moustaches.

Then I heard a voice of reason "Bernard (that's his first name), don't be a silly idiot," it's my father. I am so caught up with what was going on I didn't hear him leave the house. His calm voice breaks the mayhem, the angry mob stop and loosened their grip on Peter and his girlfriend, as do the women holding his mother, and Peter's father gets to his feet. The family all hug each other, with the father turning, pointing and shouting at Mr Bates and his 'gang', "You are nuts, you'll go to prison for this". They all walk slowly backwards, still facing the crowd, into their house. I breathe a massive sigh of relief, Mr Bates falls to his knees, starts to sob, with many of the neighbours going to comfort him. No one went over to Peter and his family to see if they were alright, I hear the police sirens coming towards the close, bet it was my mother, good for her. Mr Bates and the neighbours are bonkers.

6

This fear and anger came from punk music, music for young people, it scares the adults but the kids love it. I had no idea music could be so daring and exciting, I can't wait to be a teenager to discover the magic of music and the clothes that go with it, fashion I think they call it, yes I just can't wait.

II

A Horse, My School Dinner for a Horse

Mr Bates received a two year suspended prison sentence for disturbing the peace and criminal damage, or something like that. My father says that means he won't go to prison "as long as he's a good boy" for two years. But he should have gone to prison, he tried to kill Peter and his girlfriend. The only people interviewed by the police were the good and close friends of Ravendale Road's nut case, they weren't interested in a statement from my father or mother. I heard, when it got to court, everything favoured towards old Bates, 'cos he had more people on his side. My father told me that is how the law works, as Mr Bates is a regular church goer, loves the Queen and arranges summer fetes and jumble sales down at the Church Hall, and Judges like that, not Punk Rockers who hate the Queen. The law courts sound the same as school - adults are right, kids are wrong.

I always thought Mr Bates looked like a murderer, not that I know what a murderer looks like. Yet after watching 10 Rillington Place one Sunday night on ITV, it's a film about a real life murderer called John Christie, who murdered women in London during and after the Second World War. Like Bates, everyone thought he was a good man, and my word they don't half look the same.

Mr Bates, like Christie, is bald on top with hair round the sides and wears round steel rimmed glasses; also he wears same type suits, just like the ones you see in Dad's Army, you know the comedy show on the BBC, about the Home Guard during the war. I remember when I went to Madame Tussauds in London for a birthday treat after seeing the film, I couldn't wait to get into the Chamber of Horrors to see all those evil men and women, and when I saw the wax dummy of Christie I screamed out loud, as I thought it was Mr Bates. My mother told me to shut up, and said sorry to everyone. She asked why I screamed, I told her, she looked at the dummy, laughed and agreed with me.

Anyway that was two years ago as it's now 1979, my final year at middle school, having a great time due to my love of football. Watch Match of The Day on Saturday night, and I can't wait to chat to the 'rough boys' about the weekend's games on a Monday, be it Liverpool, Nottingham Forest, Arsenal or Man Utd first thing we talk about is football nonstop. I still support Juventus, don't really have a favourite English team, I suppose it might be West Ham, as my English grandfather supports them, but don't get upset if they lose not like when Italy loses. Italy nearly won the World Cup last year, but we lost to Holland, who were scoring these unstoppable wonder goals from outside the penalty box. They got two past Dino Zoff, and he's the best goal keeper in the world. But we came fourth in the whole championship, which was much better than England, as it was us that knocked them out. My brother tells me that we are now the fourth best team in the World, I like that, number one would have been better. I watched Italy play and beat France, Hungary and then the host nation, Argentina and eventual winners, and I must say it was the best thing I've ever seen or experienced. I would start shaking and unable to sit still from the opening of the national anthem to the referee's last blow of the whistle. It's just a shame that after the first group stages, our form dipped, a draw against West Germany, a win against Austria and then a loss, as I said, against Holland, not enough to get to the Final. We did play Brazil for the third spot, but lost that as well, but hey coming fourth is no shame. I would tease my school mates during the World Cup how England is doing, they hated that, I loved it. I was so pleased to see Bettega play and got excited by a new player called Paolo Rossi, playing up front with Bettega. Even some of the rough kids at school would sometimes shout out Rossi when they scored a goal in the playground just after the World Cup, but mainly they would shout Mario Kempes, the top Argentina goal scorer from the World Cup, I think they shouted out Rossi to make me happy as the rough boys were now my friends. My mother first of all disapproved, but after a few came round for tea and to play Subbuteo, she started to like them; I think it's their parents she doesn't like. I still read my comics but I don't tell anyone at school though, as I now play football with the rough boys, mainly in goal, and I am not bad.

In fact my performance in goal in the playground has earned me the nickname the Dino Zoff of Nursery Road. One of the rough boys, Simon White, who was good at football, as well as being liked by all the girls and every boy at school wants to be his friend, got me to go in goal for our house team, Yellow. When he told me I went to bed thinking I will be Zoff's number two at the next World Cup, and then take over his role. But my dream was short lived, I let in three goals at school, and we lost three nil. The last one went through my legs, and I kept thinking about the Scottish goalkeeper Alan Rough. Simon Brown tried to strangle me, but was pulled off by the PE teacher, Mr Sweeney, and the rest of the team. Simon and I stayed friends but I haven't been picked for Yellow House football team again.

My father got promotion and a pay rise at work last year, so he started to rent a colour TV which he got just in time for the World Cup. We had black and white for years, he's even bought my brother a record player, which he keeps in his room. My brother is now becoming more interested in music, he shuts his door when he's playing his records, I can't really make out the songs, but it sounds angry, it scares me but also makes me curious. I also noticed at the start of this year that Peter stopped wearing his punk clothes, and is dressing smart, sometimes he even looks like Napoleon Solo from The Man from Uncle. They show that a lot over the school holidays, I have even got a Man from Uncle Triangle Badge, which I haven't worn for years. Peter is wearing an old green scruffy parka, not like the ones we wear at Nursery Road. Lord Antony is the main one, dark or light blue. But I do like the way Peter looks and his girlfriend, who is called Betty, my brother found out her name. She isn't a punk anymore; she wears long black trousers with black and white tight tops, or nice skirts. She is very beautiful, she and Peter often wave to me. They didn't move out of Ravendale Road but they never talk to Mr Bates or many of the other neighbours, but they do talk to us, especially my father, as he stopped Peter from being hanged.

I love our new TV; now I can see all my favourite shows in colour. But one show I can't watch is Charlie Cairoli on the BBC, why? Good question. My father left Milan in 1956, or 57, can't remember, as he doesn't really talk about it. Anyway he wanted to be a clown or a comedian and thought England would be the place he could make it and he was following his teacher, Cairoli. My father came from a place called Affori in Italy; I think that's the correct spelling, which is near Milan, oh yea my brother supports AC Milan, not Juventus. And Charlie Cairoli and his family came from there too. His family and my family were close friends, apparently they would eat Christmas lunch together, throw birthday parties, things like that. Cairoli was older than my father and taught him a few tricks; it was what my father wanted to do. Cairoli went to England, leaving my father behind. My father worked hard on his act according to my mother and when he was 21, maybe older or younger, not quite sure, he was ready to join Cairoli. My mother said Charlie even met my father at the airport. He joined Cairoli and his assistants in Blackpool and helped to make it a huge success, even writing many of the gags, then he broke his leg and couldn't perform for six months. For no reason, or have I been told of the reason, he was sacked and Cairoli stole all his gags. My father left Blackpool, found a job, met my mother

11

and got married. For a few years he forgot about his clown friend, thinking he would never leave Blackpool then, well before I was born, Cairoli went to America and appeared on a TV show twice in November, 1962 or 1963 hosted by someone famous called Ed Sullivan, well my mother tells me he was famous, and when Charlie came back to England he became a huge star. Sad thing is, I find Charlie Cairoli funny, so does my mother. Once I was watching his show, forgetting my father was off work with a cold, he came downstairs and saw his old friend on TV and started shouting out in Italian, then in English saying "You thieving bastard of a clown, you are the son of a whore and a poof, your wife has the face of a pig and the body of a hippo and your children look like chimps!" The living room went quiet and my father went back to bed. For a few years my father would send Cairoli a Christmas card via his fan club, I don't know what he wrote but I am sure they were words like the ones he shouted at the TV. He stopped writing them when he got an official looking letter in a brown envelope, I saw my father read it, but he didn't read it out to me, he nodded, snarled and laughed, put it in his large ashtray and set fire to it with his lighter.

With the weather getting better, at school we're allowed to play on the field during lunch, morning and afternoon breaks, but we are not allowed to play football. We used to be able to, but we all came home or went to lessons covered with grass stains across our white shirts, so Mrs Titchener our headmistress banned it, but she didn't ban the girls from doing their hand stands and all that. So we just sit on the grass and chat and the other day we are standing and looking at horses in the field that backs on to our field.

Four of us, Simon White, Mickey Davies, Mark Williams and me, talking about riding a horse, then Mickey goes "It's a cinch, ridden loads of horses with me cousins in Ireland." "Never" most of us say, Mickey shakes his head, waves his hands and smiles just like a teacher.

"Easy peasy, just get on them, grab their mane, ride them bare back" The rest of us look at each other, Mickey knows everything and has done everything, reckons his grandma is a cleaner at Wembley Stadium and for the last FA Cup she let him polish the Cup before the game, or that one of his uncles was a Great Train Robber from the 60s but he never got caught. Then Simon, who's not afraid of Mickey, "Go on Mickey, get on the horse" " "Nay, got me school trousers on and me murtha will kill me". We started moving and making chicken like sounds

Mickey's face goes red, "I'll bash all of ya,",we were having too much fun to be scared by him"I'll thump ya", he shouts out as he takes swings at us, all missing as we are moving too fast, then a menacing voice, just like Darth Vader's from Star Wars, says "Get on the horse Mickey or I'll thump you", it's Nathan Swine, the toughest kid in the school. Swine only comes to school when he wants to, which makes all the teachers and kids happy, no one gets duffed up and no damage to the school is done. We are the same age but he looks and acts older, he could easily pass for sixteen. At school dinners he gets extras if he wants, we don't, but I hate school dinners anyway. He dresses loud, wears a sheep skin coat in the winter just like a football manager's and in the summer he wears a denim jacket, reminds me of David Soul from Starsky and Hutch. He always has this huge coin type gold ring on his left hand, don't know the name of the finger and he loves his slip-on brown leather boots with wavy patterns on the front, trust me a few kids have felt them up their back sides. The first day he wore them, that's all he did, and in front of the teachers as well. He's never picked on me and there is a reason.

His dad Harry is a well-known thief in Sunbury, he's been in prison a few times, and out of earshot of Nathan, we nickname him Fletcher, you know Ronnie Barker's character in Porridge, the comedy about life in prison. Harry looks like Elvis Presley, has the same haircut, wears a white vest, blue jeans, loads of gold chains round his neck and tattoos up his arm, just like my grand-father who got his when he was in the army in Burma during the Second World War. Harry goes to the pub opposite Nursery Road Middle School a lot, The Jolly Gardener, and that's how he got talking to my father. My father likes to go there on a Sunday before lunch, a lot of people don't talk to Harry, they are scared of him. But my father does, I think it's because he's different and a character as my father would say. He made my father happy as he's been to Rome a few times, I think he's the only person apart from us who has ever been to Italy. Also Harry pops round every now and then with boxes of whisky for my father, who tells me they have fallen off the back of a lorry. He sometimes stays for dinner as he always knocks when my mother is cooking. He's alright with me, winks at me and often pinches my cheek, and I suppose that is why Nathan has never picked on me, he's never talks to me he might nod, but not often. Today I am lucky as he nods at me then turns back to Mickey.

" I said to Mickey, get on the 'orse" snaps Nathan, "Leave it out Nathan…pleeze", never before have I seen my friend so petrified, but anyone would as Nathan is menacing and loves a bit of aggro. He walks forward and pulls Mickey's arm and twists it behind his back. This, and booting kids up the arse, is his party trick. Mickey starts to scream in pain "Arggh OK Nath, I will". Nathan smiles but in a sinister way and then gives Mickey a stomach punch, "me name is Nathan, not Nath", which is followed by a nut cracker on top of the head then he backs off. Mickey looking more terrified than 10 seconds ago, slowly walks to the fence, he looks back at us like a condemned man. The fence is only a foot or so taller than us, I have often wondered why the horses have never jumped over it, suppose they can't stand kids.

Mickey starts to climb up the black metal fence, and then is helped by Nathan's trade mark boot up the back side. Mickey yelps as he gets over the fence and standing in the field. Again he faces us, helpless and scared, I look at Nathan, he is enjoying this. How can anyone enjoy seeing someone else suffer? The two horses, one black and one grey, look up and stand firm, usually they just seem to mope about eating grass, then they start to snort aggressively just like Black Beauty, when she is hurt or in trouble. I must say do love that theme tune, quite magical in fact. Back to Mickey.

The horses face Mickey, and start moving their right hoofs on the ground, oh no, they are going to trample my mate to death. How am I going to explain this to the teacher after lunch, "sorry Miss, Mickey was killed by horses during lunch time." I look at Nathan, thinking maybe with a smile he might call Mickey back, saying it was all a prank. But instead he's bending over to pick up a stone, he aims and fires, bulls eye, straight on the grey horse's backside and then Nathan shouts "Hey ho Silver" just like The Lone Ranger. The horses go berserk and start galloping towards Mickey. Mickey has wasted no time and is already climbing up the fence, we all ran over to pull him back but Nathan pushes us out of the way and punches Mickey in the face, Mickey shakes his head and pulls himself up the fence, all he needs to do is to swing his legs over and he can land on the field. Nathan goes for a second punch, but Mark Williams, brave Mark hits Nathan on the side of the head and then with all his body pushes Nathan away and they start to have a fight, leaving me and Simon to grab Mickey and pull him up with all our might over the fence and we let go once we see his legs clear the fence. Mickey flies over our heads, just like Superman, he lays face down, and is groaning and crying, and at least he is alive. The horses get to the fence, and with their heads they are trying to push it down, oh shit, this will be like a disaster movie, The Swarm or Jaws, but this time two horses trampling kids to death. Mark and Nathan are fighting, Mark is certainly doing well and Nathan looks shocked, I think this the first time someone has stood up to him.

Then a man's voice shouts out "Whoa Gravy, Whoa Brambles", the two horses stop just like that, turn and trot back to the shabby looking man, just like the dad in Steptoe and Son. I fell to my knees then my back and lay next to weeping Mickey, Simon is taking deep breaths and is crouching down, whilst Mark and Nathan are still fighting. I pull myself up and see the man patting the horses and giving them a carrot each. Maybe if we scarper, mix with the other kids, just like they did in the Great Escape, we might get away with it. Mark looks happy fighting, but it's all too late, during the excitement I didn't notice we had an audience, in fact all of the kids are coming over to us to see what was going on and then the biggest bastard of them all, Mr Sweeney, appears from the crowd and straight away pulls Mark and Nathan apart and looks at me, Simon and Mickey and orders us to stay there, we oblige, we have no choice.

Steptoe comes over to the fence, Mr Sweeney walks towards him, notices he doesn't want to shake his hand, but he listens to his words "Those children of yours were throwing things (points at me and Simon, not Nathan (probably knows his dad) at my horses, one got over (points at Mickey) and even tried to kick them." I can't take this, so I shout out "Liar". The old man walks towards the fence screaming "Let me get at him". Mr Sweeney is a giant of a man, gently pushes him back, "I will deal with them, when I take them to the headmistress, I will call you" The man nods, looks at us and shakes his fist. Mr Sweeney walks over to us; we are now all on our feet and standing together, including Nathan. Mr Sweeney looks straight at Nathan, who sneakily says " Sir, Mickey and the others were teasing the horses, I tried to stop them but I couldn't, as there were four of them" Not sure if he knew Nathan was lying, either way he knew he would get the wrath of his dad Harry, so he's going for the best option for him and not the truth, "Good boy, Nathan, you can go, in fact go to the office and say Mr Sweeney said you can have a packet of crisps for being a brave boy" "Thank you sir". Nathan walks off, with Mr Sweeney facing us, he doesn't see Nathan turn round, laugh and give us the two fingers. But like Mr Sweeney none of us were going to say he was a liar, as we didn't want to face his dad as well. Seems being tough gets you very far in life. "OK boys, Mrs Titchener's office it is."

"You are cruel and spineless" screams Mrs Titchener, all four of us stand side by side, heads down and knees quivering, yet I am still overwhelmed with a sense of injustice, and as a con would say in The Sweeney "I've been fitted up". But these are adults, well teachers, and they decide if you are wrong or right, guilty or not guilty you are not allowed to say whether you are or not. Mrs

Titchener goes on to say that our lives will amount to nothing as we will end up going to the nearby Borstal in Feltham or a job at the local Airfix on the assembly line. Heard my parents say this to my brother a lot when he was doing his O 'levels. In the office is also Mr Sweeny and the horses' owner, Mr Tiles, both nodding in agreement with her words. I didn't expect this today, just wanted to come to school, see and chat with my friends, come home watch TV, play a bit of Subbuteo, not this. The yelling and screaming is nonstop, I just want this to be over and done with, why keep going on and on, we haven't killed anyone, we are children, and innocent children. My fear has now gone, I am annoyed and now getting bored. I wonder what the punishment is going to be, get perhaps a week of picking up litter or a week of clearing up horses' shit, then Mrs Titchener stops and looks at us and calmly says "I am not going to punish you". Me and my friends breathe a huge sigh, I look at Mr Sweeney and Mr Tiles who were now both standing behind Mrs Titchener, they look shocked, they can't believe their ears.

Perhaps Mrs Titchener has realised that no ill will was intended and we were boys just being boys. I even smile at her, she is stone faced, then there's a huge pause, she gazes at us with her authoritative eyes " Your peers will impose your punishment, Mr Sweeney tell all the teachers instead of a final lesson this afternoon, I want all the years in the assembly hall at 2.45 sharp. "Yes Mrs Titchener", he proudly replies. I feel like a prisoner waiting to be publically executed, just like in the French Revolution when the crowd all cheer when the guillotine comes down. I remember seeing the film The Scarlet Pimpernel and how under disguise he helped people escape from the guillotine; sadly there will be no absconding or a hero to rescue us.

The fateful hour dawns upon us, so at 2.45 PM, Mickey Davies, Simon White, Mark Williams and me all stand on the hall stage facing out towards every child and teacher in the school, even the school dinner ladies and the lollypop lady are here, oh and of course Mr Tiles is standing at the back. No one is smiling, just transfixed on us. I keep thinking all the kids are going to start shouting "off with their heads" just like in Alice in Wonderland. The minutes seem to go so slowly, how I want to get home, have some toast, read a Batman comic or watch something on TV, just to be safe and sound and away from this. The wait is over, as Mrs Titchener stands, looks at us with total disgust and turns to face her subjects. "These dirty little boys felt they needed to torture two poor defenceless horses, had it not been for the bravery of Nathan Swine, and the eagle eyes of Mr Sweeney and of course Mr Tiles, the stable owner, who knows what pain they would have caused the poor animals?" There are loud sighs and gasps; every girl looks at us with total hatred. I wasn't that popular with the girls to begin with and I am destined to be an outcast forever for something I didn't do. Whilst some of the boys, not all, have a few smiles, but many shake their heads. Nathan Swine even has the cheek to shout out "disgraceful", "Thank you Nathan, and again may I thank you on behalf of the school and Mr Tiles on saving the poor weak horses" quips Mrs Titchener. Many of the boys and girls make a point of leaning forward and patting Nathan on the back, which he clearly relishes. I look up and straight at the dinner ladies and lollypop lady, who were all snarling at us, great, now they are going to spit in my dinner and there's every chance I will get hit by a car when I cross the road, as Mrs Tubby, don't know her real name, call her that 'cos she is fat, won't hold up the lollypop sign for me anymore. We must have been up there for 45 minutes, because Mrs Titchener only stops destroying our good characters when the final bell went at 3.30 pm, my favourite sound at school.

The short walk home from school is terrible, I was alone, as Mickey, Simon and Mark all live in Upper Halliford which is the other way from me. As I slowly stroll home with my head down, I heard shouts of "horse killer, evil bastard" and such like, even a few stones whiz past my head. I seriously believe Mrs Titchener enjoyed hurting us, for me, that's far worse than what we were accused of. I love animals and took pleasure in saving Smith's crisp packets a few years ago so I could receive a collection of badges with different animals saying 'I love my pet', which I wore all of them over a course of time with pride, even though we don't own a pet, as my father has a fear of dogs, and he finds cats stupid and my mother says she doesn't want to spend her free time getting their hairs out of the carpet. We did own a gerbil once, but he died after 12 months, how I cried that day.

A few years back we went to Venice, and my father showed me the Bridge of Sighs. He told me it was used for condemned men crossing from the court to the prison, and this would be their last sight of freedom before they were put away. When I saw it I had no idea what they felt like, but now I do. I have no idea how I am going to face tomorrow, I might ask my mother if I could change schools, I've done nothing wrong, nothing, yet if a bloody teacher says you have, then everyone believes them. I am going to tell my father, he hates teachers as much as he hates policemen. Only steps away from my house, I hear a loud pop pop sound, I turn round and see Peter with Betty coming towards me on a small white motorbike, but it's not a motorbike it's a scooter, seen a lot of them when I have been on holiday in Italy and Wolfie Smith from the comedy show Citizen Smith rides one. My father tells me they make them in Italy and sell them all over the world. My uncle, who lives in Milan, has one in the garage, but it's old and rusty, I sometimes sit on it with my cousins and make sounds like the pop pop one, but this is the first scooter I have seen in England, well Sunbury anyway. Peter looks smart, not Man from Uncle suit smart with his green parka, but blue jeans and a white tee shirt with a circle on it with words going round it, as he is moving can't read it all, but I can make out two, The Jam. The Jam? Who or what are the Jam, and Betty looks beautiful as ever, dressed like my mother and her friends did before I was born, seen the photos, so that's how I know. As we make eye contact Peter gives me a big smile and Betty blows me a kiss, a kiss, I am in love with her and the scooter. If having a scooter means I get a girlfriend like her, then I will get one when I get older.

I have forgotten about the trouble today at Nursery Road I just want to know what The Jam is. Half an hour or so later, my brother comes in from school, well he's left school but at the sixth form, who wants to stay on at school when you don't have to. My father says it's because he doesn't want to work in the real world. As he comes in, I ask him " What's The Jam", he laughs and goes upstairs, what did I say that was so funny, then he comes downstairs and gives me an LP, The Jam, All Mod Cons. Of course it's a band, I look at the front cover, three men in a big room. One is standing and two are sitting down, the dark haired one in the middle scares me as he looks evil, reminds me of Christopher Lee as Dracula, whilst the fair haired one sitting down with a cigarette looks friendly and the other one with dark hair standing, looks like he likes a good fight. They all look smart, just like Peter dresses and even my brother does now, which is better than before, as he always used to look like Worzel Gummidge, in fact my brother is dressing like my uncle does in Milan. I like the way The Jam look, not as scruffy as in the photos of the punk bands I have seen or as stupid like those glam bands, Gary Glitter, Sweet, Mud and shit like that. "Come up, and I will play you the LP", we exchange smiles; it's been a long time since we have really chatted.

In his room, he blows the needle and puts the record on, a few scratches then I hear a voice "1, 2, 3, 4" then this loud powerful music starts, I can make out guitar, bass and drums followed by this aggressive and passionate voice singing "Seen you before, I know your sort, You think the world awaits your every breath", my word they are singing about my head mistress Mrs Titchener. From being made an outsider by my school, then seeing a scooter and hearing this music, I am happy and proud, I don't care what they think of me at school, I have just discovered a new band….. The Jam

III

Destination Known

School is OK, I am not totally isolated from my 'school mates', just the kids I didn't really talk to anyway. The 'rough boys' knew what really happened and in fact it created a bond between us and the teachers. 'Us against them' as my father would say. Saw a play on the BBC a while back called Smike, based on a Charles Dickens' book Nicholas Nickleby, it was a few years ago. There was a scene where Nickleby, seeing some kids being beaten and bullied by a teacher with a cane, grabs the cane, breaks it over his knee and the kids start to rebel. Hope it happens one day here at Nursery Road. Us taking on Mr Sweeney and Mrs Titchener, God how I hate her. I can't understand why she got a job working with children, as she seems to dislike us, well that's not true, she likes the ones that are well behaved and boring, and her 'informers', Vanessa Mills and Stuart Southgate, head girl and head boy. Southgate tried to play football with us, but he gave up as no one passed to him. He spends his playground break speaking to Mills and her friends, whilst looking at us playing football. My father says he will become a policeman, I can't understand why any kid would rather be on the side of the teachers than us, can't stand him, never have.

Football isn't our only thing now, we are talking about music a lot, especially on a Friday morning after Top of The Pops. As I said, before it was only the girls who, to me, seem to be into music, shit like David Cassidy, David "Bleeding" Essex and David Soul, but since punk there are bands for the boys too. We often sing Oliver's Army, talk about how tough The Stranglers look, how beautiful Debbie Harry is from Blondie and how Squeeze's Cool for Cats is about having it off. The one that everyone talks about is The Sex Pistols' Friggin' in the Riggin, many of the kids knows the lyrics off by heart 'Twas on the good ship Venus, By Christ you should have seen us, the figurehead was a whore in bed, And the mast a rampant penis ". Singing the song is totally banned, which I love, as it scares and annoys the teachers. Mickey Davies was singing it the other day in the hall whilst queuing up for school dinner. Southgate, just like Mr Mackay the prison warder from Porridge, tried to order him to stop. Ole' Mickey punched him straight in the mouth, we all cheered, well the rough boys did, and I was pleased some of the girls did as well, but not Mills and her friends they all screamed. Mickey got the cane but loads of pats on the back from us, he loved it, he was a hero again especially after Nathan Swine had bullied him, I'll come to him in a minute. The following day, Mrs Titchener in Morning Assembly, told us about the evils of modern music, and how wonderful music once was, then with the old school record player she played some Glen Miller records. I think I was the only one who knew who he was, as my English grandfather loves Glen Miller, plays records when we are over there, but never at Christmas, that's always The Beatles thanks to my uncle. Saw the film about him, called The Glen Miller Story, believe it or not and how he went missing after he went up in a plane, he was never found or the plane. She played Moonlight Serenade, heard the song a lot, my grandfather's favourite. I looked round to see the faces of the other kids, many looked bored, but the ones like Southgate and Mills, were swaying their heads in time to the music. When the record stopped, before old Titchener could say a word I shouted out "They never found his body".

Now if Southgate had said that she would have agreed with him, but no, not me, I was sent out of the hall and told to wait outside her office, I was really getting used to this. Got the usual boring lecture from her, no cane or punishment, just told me the same shit as before I would never amount to anything, ' Feltham Borstal or the local Airfix factory'. Heard a record the other day called Borstal Breakout, by a band called Sham 69. What a song, fast, angry and powerful. My brother says they live nearby, a place called Hersham, near Walton-on-Thames; it has a good toy shop there.

I said I would get to Nathan Swine. He left school just like that, went to work, believe it or not, at some stables in Staines, owned by his uncle. After the incident with the horses, I told my parents the truth, as did Mickey and the others, whose parents all went down the school to complain about our mistreatment. Even my father had a chat with Harry, his dad remember, over a pint one Sunday down The Jolly Gardeners. Harry was upset that I was punished, well that's what my father told me, and gave Nathan a clout. But he didn't want to be shown up at school, so he went, I think Mrs Titchener felt the same, easier to let him go than for her to say sorry to us in front of the whole school.

My brother is buying loads of records, that's how I heard Borstal Breakout. He's got a Saturday job, and during the school holidays at Blades the Butcher's at Sunbury Cross, and he buys the records from a shop at the Cross called Record Scene. My parents work, they and my brother don't usually get home until about 5ish, 'cos of the travel and the buses, so I am left on my own, which I love. Used to go home and watch TV, but now it's straight up to his room and play his records, and the ones I love and play the most, is The Jam.

Like when I discovered horror films, I wanted to learn all about them. For my birthday and Christmas I would get books about them, I'd go to my bedroom and read about all the Universal and Hammer films, the actors, the plots, the directors, be it Todd Browning or Terence Fisher. There wasn't one kid at Nursery Road who knew as much as me. I love to learn things, not what the teachers tell me, what I want to know, I know I am clever but not in the school's eyes. It's the same with The Jam, after my brother played me All Mods Cons, I pulled out the inner sleeve read all the words. I can now sing along to every song on the LP without having the words nearby, or the 'lyrics' as my brother would correct me. See that Paul Weller, the Dracula lookalike, writes all the songs, he writes brilliant songs, and on the other side of the sleeve there are all these images, on top a diagram of a scooter, another band called The Creation, something called SKA, some nice photos of The Jam, a Union Jack badge, I hope they don't like The Royal Family, some nice dark glasses (saw Peter the other day wearing some glasses like these) a packet of Rothmans cigarettes. When I buy my first packet of cigarettes I am going to make sure they are Rothmans, there's loads of things on there. The other two are called Bruce Foxton, the one who looks as though he likes a fight, plays bass, and the friendly looking one is Rick Buckler, he plays the drums. My brother says they come from Woking, which is nearby. I have never heard of it or been there. So we have Sham 69 and The Jam coming from the same area as me, I never really thought about where bands came from. I know The Beatles come from Liverpool, first time I heard the town Liverpool was a song by Jimmy Osmond called Long Haired Lover from Liverpool, I hated it, all the girls used to sing and dance to it, and I never remember Mrs Titchener telling them to shut up. Their football team seems to be the best in England and Europe, used to have Kevin Keegan, everyone loved him, well apart from Marco Tardelli, he elbowed Keegan straight in the jaw when Italy played England at Wembley in November 1977. He knocked Keegan out, I loved it, then 10 minutes later Tardelli got Keegan booked, brilliant.

My brother has now bought all The Jam's records; singles and LP's. Love them all, when I hear their music it seems like they have suffered the same as me, - "I've learned more than you'll ever know, Even at school I felt quite sure, That one day I would be on top, And I'd look down upon the map."

A lyric from This is A Modern World, Weller and his friends hate

24

teachers just as much as me. When I saw The Jam for the first time on Tops of The Pops playing Strange Town, I was just as excited as when I saw Italy play in the 1978 World Cup. The Jam played twice on the show doing Strange Town, but my favourite was all of them in these colourful striped jackets and Paul Weller wearing dark glasses, I want to wear a jacket and glasses like that. They dress so smart, and look like the 'rough kids' I play football with, but older and tougher. Their look, my brother tells me, is Mod and my brother says he is a Mod now. From what I've learnt, the first Mods were from the sixties, wore suits, rode scooters, had green parkas and listened to good music. My brother might be a Mod, but Peter is smarter and now I talk to him and beautiful Betty about The Jam. When I first started singing, very badly may I say, Down at the Tube Station at Midnight, Peter was impressed so was Betty, who kissed me on the cheek and said I was adorable, made my day. I think I am in love. Peter has seen The Jam play, I want to see The Jam play and dress like them, I want to be a Mod, I am going to be a Mod. But first I'd better ask my mother if I can have my birthday present early, so I can get some new clothes to become a Mod.

I haven't asked my mother for my early birthday present yet, heard her and my father talking about household bills that needed to be paid, so I will have to wait. Been doing this for years, know when to ask, they say they will think about it, a day or so later say yes, take me shopping usually to Kingston, a town nearby with loads of good shops, buy my present and tell me not to expect anything for my birthday, I say I won't and how grateful I am, then come my birthday, I get a present. One of my aunts says I have charm, not sure what that means, but if it means I get things I want in a crafty way, then I like it.

Made a new friend, Mark Jones, known him since primary school, always chatted but just a passing chat, but saw him come into school the other day with a smart kidlike parka on, I want one, it had a few badges on it, some pinned and some sewed, The Jam, and The Who, heard of The Who, but never heard their music, but if Jones is wearing their name, they must be good. I went

25

up to Mark in the corridor the other day just as the bell was ring-
ing for morning break and said " I love The Jam and I am a Mod",
he replied rather cheekily "you've got a long way to go, what songs
do you like, do you like 'A' Bomb?" I think he was trying to catch
me out, so I started singing

"I'm stranded on the vortex floor, My head's been kicked in
and blood's started to pour, Through the haze I can see my girl,
Fifteen geezers got her pinned to the door."

He smiles and sings "There's an 'A' bomb in Wardour Street,
it's blown up the City" then we carry on with the rest of the song,
he starts jumping up and down on the spot, I follow him. Mickey
Davies, always one not to miss out on the fun, joins in, he doesn't
know all the words, but he loves the jumping. Many of the kids
walk past us some smiling, some looking scared, fuck them. Since
listening to The Jam I like swearing more, sure my mother will dis-
approve. Yet again, as always at school, our joy is short lived, Mrs
Titchener storms out of her office, screams out for Mr Sweeney
and Mr Wilson, who in a flash are by her side, just like Batman
and the Bat signal with Commissioner Gordon. In case you didn't
know, when he needs Batman, he shines a beam into the skyline
of Gotham City with a symbol of a bat, and The Caped Crusader
is there within seconds, well unless he's fighting The Joker or The
Riddler of course. Sweeney and Wilson grab us, while Sweeney
gets hold of Mark and Mickey and Wilson gets hold of me and we
are marched to her office. Mr Wilson, he's OK, the only teacher in
school I like. He whispers in my ear "don't answer back; say sorry
and you should be OK" as we enter into the 'torture chamber'.

Our punishment again was judgement by our peers, this time it
was the next morning's assembly where Mrs Titchener was telling
the staff and pupils how she had caught us jumping up and down
like Zebedee from the Magic Roundabout and singing like stray
cats. All the rough boys, and even some girls smiled, that makes
me happy. The usual ones gave us disapproving stares, along with
the dinner ladies. But this time, I am proud, then she makes us
perform yesterday's act, Mark, Mickey and I exchange glances,

but we start jumping up and down singing 'A' Bomb in Wardour Street, with Mickey joining in the chorus, as he doesn't know all the words. No fucking teacher is going to destroy my love for The Jam. Mrs Titchener is shocked, as she sees us enjoying ourselves, and this time, the school was mixed, not everyone hates us. She has lost and we have won, my first victory against a teacher, I am Marco Tardelli, I am Paul Weller, I am a Mod.

Mark and I have become good mates, I often go to his house after school for dinner, he sometimes comes to mine, he likes the pasta my mother serves, a lot of the other kids don't like 'foreign muck'. I think they just eat burger, chips, beans and eggs all the time yak. I love salami, Italian cheeses and olives. Mark's mum is an OK cook, likes to do chops. But I am not interested in the food, he has a scrap book with cuttings of The Jam, The Who, which I read whilst he plays some records, he has a record player in his room along with a portable TV, my word. His dad is a milkman, my father, who does know him, says every week is a Christmas bonus for Mark's father. I guess that means he fiddles his takings. Mark has cuttings on other bands, new ones I have never heard of or seen on Top of The Pops, The Chords, The Purple Hearts, Secret Affair and ones from the sixties, The Kinks, The Small Faces. Even though his dad might be a dishonest milk man, he was a Mod in the sixties, and tells us about growing up in Paddington before he moved down to Sunbury. I always thought Paddington was the name of a bear. I come home amazed with all this new music I have learnt about. I still haven't asked for my birthday present as my mother and father are planning to have the house painted, not a good time. So I might not look like a Mod yet but I have the heart of one, shame my brother's clothes don't fit me.

My brother, along with Peter and Mark's older brother, Wayne, went to a pub near Waterloo train station to see one of these new Mod bands, The Chords. Oh I wish I was older, had a job to buy clothes and records, go and see bands like The Jam, The Chords and loads more, have a scooter and take a girl like Betty out. Being a child is so cruel; you aren't allowed to do anything. I always thought Waterloo was a song by Abba, but after being clipped by my brother for saying that, he told me it was a battle between the Duke of Wellington and Napoleon over a 100 years ago I think, named a train station after it and the pub they go to is called The Wellington named after The Duke. I would be lying to say I go to London a lot, but I have been a few times with my parents and the school, I do like it. I also have a book called This is London with great drawings of London, and with a drawing of a Queen's Guard on the cover, read it so many times, looks a great place, my mother always tells me a lot about London.

I was there a few months back with our favourite teacher Mr Wilson, the one I just told you about. A school outing to Pudding Lane and to walk up the steps of The Monument, it's where the Great Fire of London started in 1666. On the way back with my usual friends, we saw a couple of lads with long hair. I think long hair looks so stupid, all those bands in platform soled boots and glitter, silly music.

I shout out "Get yer haircut", they chase us, I didn't think they would or just give up, oh no, they chase us all the way to the coach nearby. Mr Wilson and a young pretty teacher Miss Russell, who is always giggling round Mr Wilson and hugging him, were there waiting for all the kids, I ran towards him pleading for his help. Mr Wilson looked stunned, yet quickly saw we were in trouble. We all stood behind him, one of the long haired yobbos shouted "get out of the way grandad" and tried to punch Mr Wilson, but he ducked. Mr Wilson is a former boxer and ex-soldier, so he knows how to fight. Mr Wilson threw a punch and one of the long haired yobs went down, we all cheered including Miss Russell. The other yobbo who thought he was tough tried to fight Mr Wilson, it lasted about two minutes as he was knocked down as well. Again we all applauded, Miss Russell was jumping up and down, she was enjoying it. The police quickly turned up, took Mr Wilson to one side, he came back smiling and the police took the long haired yobbos away, once they had recovered. It seems policemen and teachers stick together

Someone must have told Mrs Titchener. How I hate kids telling tales to teachers when it has nothing to do with them. A few of us were called to her office, but nothing was done as we told her and kept telling her we were chased for no reason. Mr Wilson told her we were telling the truth. She didn't want to believe it, but this time we received no punishment, but we weren't asked if we were OK.

I will be leaving Nursery Road School soon, sad to go in a way, but looking forward to becoming a teenager, get a part time job and become a true Mod. My brother, father and mother all say we are heading for a bad time, as the other week Great Britain voted for a new prime minster, the first woman ever, Margaret Thatcher, she doesn't half remind me of Mrs Titchener. My father isn't allowed to vote, he's allowed to stay in the country, but my brother and mother seem to like the Labour party, and I've been reading about it. I like the concept of fairness to all people not just the rich. I will vote labour when I am old enough to vote.

Had a half day at school today, don't know why, a teacher's meeting or something. My father says they have a party in the staff room, I think he is right as all the teachers seem keen for the lunch time bell as much as the children. Can't be bothered to go out on my bike, play football or go round a friend's house, fancy reading for a change. My brother gave me a book called Animal Farm by George Orwell about farm animals led by pigs overthrowing the farmer and creating an equal society for them all. Like the idea of that, us taking over the school and equality for us, I would have Mrs Titchener clean the toilets. I see Mr Bates as I walk towards my front door, we look at each other, no hello or swear words, just staring, but he scares me. Wondering if he's plotting to murder me or the whole family.

I am finding it hard to read as I can't stop thinking about Mr Bates. I look out of my bedroom window and see him, his wife, she's another one who reminds me of Margaret Thatcher, and his two daughters, who hate me even more so since I was wrongly accused of trying to torture those horses. They are getting into his old car, which looks like it is from the Second World War, they are dressed smart, in their way, not the Mod smart way. Looks like they are going to meet the Queen, I am laughing because of the prank I pulled two years ago, but I can never tell anyone. I'm friends with Peter and Betty now, he promised he will take me out on his scooter over the summer, Mark is dead jealous. I can't read, I need to do something else, I fancy having a look round the Bates' garden.

Over the years, I've learnt how to creep out of the house, and have a wander round my neighbours gardens, don't know why I do it, but I find it fun. I started it just before I drew moustaches on the Queen's photos. My parents would go out once a week and my brother would be doing something, so I would go out, walk round the close, each time would push myself and find myself in someone's back garden. I have never stolen or damaged anything, just walk round and climb back over the gate. But I ain't done it for a while and I think Mr Bates' garden needs a wander, been too scared before as he would probably kill me. But I now like teasing and annoying adults, especially horrible adults like him and his wife.

I've changed into my outdoor clothes, old jeans and tee-shirt, not something Pete Townsend from The Who would wear. Climbing over his side gate is easy, and his garden is like something I could see the Queen sitting in, the grass is so green, not down trodden like ours, beautiful flowers, and well cut trees and bushes, hate to say it, it's lovely, really beautiful. OK, seen it, let's go back and do some reading, as my brother's bound to ask me questions about Animal Farm.

Hold on, he's got his back upper kitchen window open, I could easily squeeze through that, I am small for my age and often reminded of that. I've got to do it, a dare to myself, I've got to see his house. I give one final look round before I enter, no one is around. Been a good climber, since family holidays in Norfolk, climbed trees a lot, my father says I must have been born a monkey. Manage to get inside easily, slowly ease myself down to the

Bates' kitchen sink and pull my legs through the window. I need a cloth to wipe any footprints or marks, not surprised to see Mrs Bates has one right by the kitchen sink. The kitchen is spotless, and again nice, on the fridge is a board with a black marker pen clipped to it, it has all the things they need to buy. Surprised my mother hasn't got one as she loves writing our shopping list. I'm never asked what I want, just have to eat what is given to me, well I don't work so that's fair enough. I can't believe what I see, photos upon photos, some framed, others just nicely stuck on the wall of The Royal Family, especially The Queen. I walk out of the kitchen into their dining room, loads there, into the hallway, covered in them, and their front room is totally, utterly, like a shrine to Her Majesty, this is madness, the man is totally and utterly obsessed with ER II. I can't just leave, I need to tease him, Peter and Betty are out, I think Peter goes to college and Betty works in Shepperton, not sure what, never asked her and she's never told me. So he can't harm them.

In less than five minutes I have returned Mr Bates to his nightmare of 1977 and drawing moustaches on any photos I could of the Queen. With more time I am able to draw a few beards with some glasses, he will go bonkers, crazy. I've got to go before I start laughing. Better quickly put the pen back, wipe any prints off, get back, have some toast and wait for the fun to begin. Leaving the house via the front door easy, no one sees a thing, perhaps if I don't get a well-paid job I could steal from people's houses, but I think I will try and form a band first, or became an actor.

My mother will be home soon, better look busy as she seems to know when I've been naughty. Time has moved slowly, everyone is home now, I mean my home, not Mr Bates'. It's dinner time, we call it dinner, not tea like the rough boys do and we call lunch, lunch, not dinner like the rough boys do. I do sometimes say dinner and tea, my mother goes mad when I do. I am just about to tuck into my Shepherd's Pie, my mother's gone English tonight, and she makes a nice one, when I hear "You fucking bastards, how dare you, how fucking dare you", Oh boy he's back and he's mad, like it. My father shakes his head, my brother looks confused and my mother looks at me, "Why are you looking at me".

Before she can answer, my father is by the window, "You'd better come and see this", there's Mr Bates in his white shirt, waistcoat, John Christie trousers and his smart brown shoes, swinging a spade, he looks insane, surprised he doesn't turn green in a second and become The Hulk, "you're fucking bastards, every one of you". Instead of going to Peter's house, he goes to another neighbour's smashes their front window with the spade, my word this is brilliant, I am watching him with amusement as well as feeling the gaze of my mother, she knows, oh shit. The whole street comes out as it's dinner time for us all, no one ever phones or knocks on the door between seven to eight. No one dares to go near him as he will surely kill them.

Bugger this, I am going to call the police, the man is dangerous" says my father, but someone must have beaten him to it, as I hear the police sirens screeching up. Bet the police are pleased, can't really see them being that busy on an early summer's evening in Sunbury. He must have smashed at least another three windows and two cars rear windows before he is wrestled to the ground, then taken away by the police. This time all the neighbours look shaken up. I mean, a supposedly upstanding member of the road smashing windows with a spade is not what you expect to see during dinner time, total and utter beautiful madness. I love this, my second great prank, better than the last. But before I face the wrath of my mother I sing to myself

If you see me in the street - look away, 'Cause I don't ever want to catch you looking at me - Mr. Clean, 'Cause I hate you and your wife, And if I get the chance I'll fuck up your life".

Well said The Jam.

IV

Only When I Laugh

As my grandmother often says "it's the final straw that breaks the camel's back", and that's what happened with my father too, he had had enough, said it was time to move. OK it was me who pushed Mr Bates to the edge, but I didn't think he was Norman Bates from Psycho. Well deep down I knew he wasn't quite right in the head, a good man on a Sunday in Church, but behind the net curtains, a nutter, just like John Christie. So my father has put the house on the market and made an offer on a house in Walton-on-Thames over the river. As I said a while back, love the toy shop there and opposite is a nice fish and chip restaurant you can sit down in, my father and mother love it there. In fact, only the other weekend, ITV showed a modern horror film called Psychomania, about a gang of boys and girls who ride around on motorcycles, causing trouble. The leader makes a pact with the devil, kills himself and comes back from the dead, indestructible, just like Captain Scarlet. The leader said as long as you believe you can come back you will, and it was all filmed round Walton-on-Thames. I'd like to make a pact like that and cause mayhem. My brother told me that they were bikers, sworn enemies of The Mods. They were certainly scruffy with long hair. My brother is looking forward to moving to Walton-on-Thames, 'cos of Sham 69 coming from Hersham, which is part of my new town, reckon their lead singer Jimmy Pursey still lives there. Wonder if Paul, Bruce and Rick still live in Woking, be great if they do.

The final week at Nursery Road was a bit of a non-event, no goodbye party, just a few of us signing each other's books, going to miss Mickey, Simon, Mark and the others but not the teachers. My mother says I will make new friends as I am young. But it took me years to make friends in Sunbury, going to miss Peter and Betty as well, Peter said he would come over and give me that promised ride on his scooter. Betty, oh beautiful Betty, looked sad to see me go. The police questioned Peter about the 'vandalism', but he was at college and everyone saw him there, I was never questioned, not sure if I can handle the police - well not yet. My mother stills thinks, well knows, it was me who broke into Mr Bates 'house and drew moustaches on his photos of the Queen. But due to me going before Mrs Titchener every other week, I have become a good liar, yet she can tell. Deep down she probably finds it funny, as she couldn't stand him either.

As for Mr Bates, he went straight to prison, don't know how the law works but as I told you, he had a 2 year suspended sentence and my father says that it lasts for two years, so he had to be a good boy during this period. But he didn't, if I had done the 'vandalism' a month later he would have been OK, but he was under watch, so thanks to me he will be spending the next two summers and Christmas' in prison, makes ya laugh don't it, bet he's already joined the prison's Church choir.

Only spent two weeks of the summer holiday in Sunbury before we moved to a nice new estate, Egmont. Some of the houses haven't been finished, but I do like it. It's new and bright, has a modern feel to it, All Mod Cons, any excuse to quote The Jam. My mother has put my chopper bike under lock and key, as she doesn't want me cycling to Sunbury on the busy roads to see my old friends. She's told me I will have to walk as it's safer and I will see more. Told my mother, as we have moved, might be an idea if I had some new clothes, she said she would think about it, which means I have to behave myself for a few weeks, if not, no new clothes. But if I meet new Mods I want to look smart, like The Jam or The Who. I am wearing bleeding Wizz kid trainers from Woolworths, cheap jeans from Tesco's, and old tee shirts, I have no idea where they came from.

With my mother and father out at work, my brother still going to Sunbury on the bus to work at Blades the Butcher's, I am left in the house on my own and today is a beautiful summer's day, too nice to be watching TV, listening to music or reading. So I am going to go out and see if there are any Mods about, even though I have these horrible green trainers on, wouldn't see Rick Buckler in these, no way. The town centre is only ten minutes' walk from my new house, and my mother was right, I do see more; it is very green and seems to have more character than Sunbury. Sunbury is nice, well Sunbury Cross where all the shops are is a bit rough, with a tower block nearby, it has an underpass and when I used to walk through with my mother, she would often say she wouldn't like to walk there late at night.

Never walked round Walton town centre on my own before, loads more shops than Sunbury, even see a record shop, just like Record Scene in Sunbury, but this one is called Tower Records. As I walk past, two Mods come out, brilliant, new friends. They are both wearing parkas. Its summer, they must be baking. They have a few badges and patches, one is wearing blue Sta Press trousers and the other is wearing brown Tonic trousers, both have white Fred Perry's. Even though my brother is dressing smart, it was Peter and Mark who told me all about Sta Press, Tonic suits, Fred Perry's, Ben Sherman button down shirts, Hush Puppies and Levis Jeans. Bet Paul Weller has got a wardrobe full of Mod clothing, even two. I have made a list of the clothes I want. One of the Mods is wearing dark glasses, just like Rick Buckler has on In The City album; want one of those smart black suits like The Jam wear. I say hello to the Mods, they look at me, look at each other than laugh, my face goes red.

Slightly embarrassed I go into Tower Records, my word it's like Aladdin's Cave, posters of all the good bands and records everywhere, The Jam, Sham 69, Squeeze, The Stranglers, Blondie, The Clash and all these new bands. Behind the counter are two teenagers, who smile at me, the record they are playing sounds good, a catchy number Here Comes The Summer, I recognise the voice and the sound, a band that did Jimmy Jimmy, the singer with a strange but interesting voice, it's The Undertones, I am getting good, I can recognise a band straight away. To show my new found knowledge I shout out "Is that the Undertones' new single?" The shop boys seem impressed, I am very happy. My mother did leave me some money to 'treat myself', but not enough to treat myself to a Fred Perry. Anyway I buy my first single, The Undertones, Here Comes the Summer, I am so happy and proud. They might not be a Mod band, but the song sounds quite Mod. My brother will be dead proud. I say goodbye and tell the staff at Tower Records I will be back to buy more singles, and I will. I am liking Walton more and more. Then I hear "stop thief", I turn round thinking that someone is shouting out at me, instead I see a young boy about my age, even looks Italian, dark hair and dark eyes, with dark skin, like me, but not so skinny.

The boy seems to be laughing, and as he comes closer to me I can see he's holding loads of chocolate bars, we exchange glances, rather cheekily he says "watcha ". I've got to follow this kid, so I start running beside him, I look over my shoulder and see a rather red faced fat man chasing us. Oh it's been a long time since I've been in trouble, how I've missed it, my mother and father did say they 'wanted me to turn over a new leaf', oh yeah I will, but it doesn't necessarily mean it will be a good leaf, perhaps a naughtier one. The boy winks at me as we run across the road, cars slamming their brakes on, bleeping their horns, a few adults try and grab us, but we are too fast, so they give up.

I feel like I am in a Laurel and Hardy film, this boy is laughing, I mean really laughing. I fall back a bit and allow him to lead, as I don't know the area that well. We turn right at the High Street, run up a small hill, hit a left down a nice small but winding road which widens at the end. Looking over my shoulder again I see we have lost the fat red faced man. The boy nods his head for me to follow him. I've always been told not to go with strangers, but there is something about him. He leads me to a small park, and we are by the river. He sits down, I do as well, he chucks me a Dairy Milk bar, one of my favourites, I open it up and start eating. "You're now handling stolen goods, you could go to prison for that, hope your father can afford a good lawyer laddie", chips the Italian looking boy.

Straight away I laugh, he asks my name and how come I was in Walton High Street, so I tell him who I am and how I've just moved to Walton "So the first friend you make is a thief, a good start", which was followed by mad laughing, just like The Joker from Batman, this kid is potty, but I like him, and pleased he called us friends. Then it dawned on me, this poor boy must be poor or even homeless, that's why he's stealing. Surely my mother will allow him to stay for a few days, have a hot meal, a bath, a nice bed and we could help find him somewhere to live. " If you want a proper meal, and even a bed, I only live 10 minutes away, we could even watch some TV and play some records" The boy looks at me bewildered, I think he is touched by my act of human kindness, but no, he has a fit of hysteria, rolls about on the grass, laughing with tears running down his cheeks, eventually he calms down, wiping the tears from his eyes, "Thanks for the offer, but I am not a pauper but a prince". He must have seen the same TV programme as me a few years ago, based on a book, The Prince and The Pauper, written by Mark Twain. Read The Adventures of Tom Sawyer by him, liked that a lot, kids about my age, having fun and adventures in the summer.

My new friend dips into his jeans pocket, must say they look a nicer pair of jeans than the cheap Tesco ones I have got on, he pulls out a big blue five pound note, and I thought my mother was being generous by giving me a pound note this morning. I am often given a five pound note at Christmas or my birthday from an aunt or uncle but never allowed to take it out with me, my mother or father always take it and say they will look after it, otherwise I will spend it all at once, which to me is the whole idea. So I have to see something I like, then ask for the money, only then I am given the five pound note and my father always insists on a receipt and the change. He tells me he is teaching me the value of money, but this kid has a whole five pound note to himself. Maybe he has stolen the money as well, oh my God, he's the Artful Dodger, you know the top pickpocket from Oliver Twist, I would like to be able to pickpocket. After watching Oliver one Christmas I tried to pickpocket a few relatives who were over for the festive season, I was useless, got caught every time, they found it funny, well my mother and father didn't, but if I hadn't been caught I would have kept their money.

Perhaps this boy will teach me the art of stealing, "Wow, where did you steal that money from?", again the boy starts laughing, he is totally bonkers, never met anyone who laughs so much, and over nothing. It lasts for about five minutes before he can reply, "I didn't steal the money, it's my pocket money" His pocket money? Then he must be the son of a millionaire. "Why did you steal the chocolate bars?, I am confused, he could afford to buy these sweets. "Because I was bored and I wanted some fun" he quirkily replies. I can understand that, life can be boring without annoying an adult, I like him even more, he's been laughing so I haven't even asked his name where he is from, his age or what school he goes to, but I only want to know one thing,"Are you a Mod?, I am a Mod", He looks at me, this time he doesn't laugh " I thought Mods are meant to be smart, you look like the Bisto Kid" That's it, this weekend I am begging my mother to take me clothes shopping, had enough of wanting to be a Mod, but looking like some orphan kid from Victorian London, " I am going shopping this weekend to get my new Fred Perry's and Tonic trousers, just like Paul Weller"

"Who?"

"Paul Weller from The Jam"

"Paul Welling?"

"No Weller"

"He can't sing and The Jam are a punk band."

No, they are not and he can sing."

"Yea like an alley cat in a bad mood, no, I am not a Mod, I like good music, my mother likes The Beatles and my father likes Frank Sinatra, Dean Martin".

"So you like what your parents tell you to like, what about The Stranglers, The Clash, The Undertones, Blondie?"

He smiles "I like Blondie, I like Debbie Harry", and that's it, he likes them because of their beautiful singer. My brother has a big poster of Debbie Harry on his bedroom wall. We talk more, he doesn't really seem interested in music, football or comics, just having fun and being naughty. Then he looks at his smart watch, and says "better go, my mother wants me back home for tea" He smiles, gets up says goodbye and goes, just like Batman. I didn't get to ask his name, yet I am sure I will see him again, I just know it.

I feel like Peter Parker, after he has been bitten by the radioactive spider. I am standing in my bedroom looking at myself in the mirror, in my new Tonic trousers, blue Fred Perry, OK it's not a Fred Perry, but we found a shop in Kingston that did Fred Perry type shirts and my suede shoes, couldn't find any Hush puppies, but these look dead smart, Rustlers they are called. I like Kingston, first time ever been clothes shopping there for me, not for school uniform or toys. Found some great shops Mancini and Jack Brendon who had loads of Mod clothes, for all ages, as well as some other shops, also found Books, Bits and Bobs, which had loads of badges, got a few The Jam, The Who and one of the new Mod bands, Secret Affair, still haven't heard their music yet. Books, Bits and Bobs has also got loads of Batman and Spiderman comics, which my mother added to the basket. She took the day off work to get my new clothes, after she found me crying in my bedroom telling her everyone was calling me a tramp as I walked through Walton. It's been years since I've done the crying trick, thought I was too old for it, but it worked and here I am looking like the younger brother of Paul Weller. I am now a Mod and so pleased to chuck those bloody Wizz Kid trainers away. My mother told me not to expect anything for my birthday, which is October or for Christmas, but as you know and I know, I will get a present.

It's now August, and England seems to be Mod mad. The Jam have a new single out called When You're Young, sounds like it was written for me, and I must say love Secret Affair's Time for Action. My brother bought it the other day, I haven't stopped playing it, it's all about a Mod revolution coming. Remember reading about The Russian Revolution, like the idea of getting rid of The Royal Family and letting the people take over, I think Mod is a revolution. And I keep hearing an advert on the radio for a new film called Quadrophenia by The Who, all about Mods. My brother went to see the film, it's an X certificate, which means no chance of me getting into the cinema, never been allowed in the cinema unless I am with my parents or my brother. My brother tells me that the story is all about Jimmy the Mod and his friends, living around London, somewhere called Shepherd's Bush, fighting Rockers and going to Brighton on their scooters and how at the end, after Jimmy's friend stops talking to him, he crashes his scooter, then he steals a scooter and rides it to the cliffs, he says you see the scooter go over the edge but not Jimmy.

Even without seeing the film I feel inspired, but I can't wait to see it. Got a book the other day from WH Smith, well got two, well my brother did, The Who in Their Own Words and The Beatles in Their Own Words, read both of them in a day. Not having any new friends yet means I have a lot of time reading and my parents don't like me walking round Walton every day, they said the neighbours will think I am a latch key kid, whatever that means. Fuck the neighbours, but I best listen to my parents.

But now I do know a lot about The Who and The Beatles, even though The Beatles aren't a Mod band, but I love their clothes and their music, they did dress like Mods sometime before they had long hair and beards, hippies is what I think they are called. I don't like that look, and The Who have another film out, all about them, The Kids Are Alright, my brother has seen that and bought the LP to go with it, listen to that a lot. I like The Who, so angry, powerful, loud and, like The Beatles, they dress like hippies after a few years of being smart. I hope I don't become a hippy, hope it's not a cycle or something, you become a Mod, dress smart, then dress scruffy. From reading about them it seems to have a lot to do with drugs, if drugs want to make you dress so badly, then why do them? My brother also buys all the music papers, NME, Melody Maker and Sounds, which has an article written by someone called Garry Bushell. Sounds like he is a Mod, he knows all about what is going on and how it started. He calls it a Mod Renewal, not a revival, like that term, even the Mod renewal or revival has made the Sunday papers, read a piece on it in the Observer or The Times, can't remember as my father took it to work to read and left it there.

Bushell says some young Mod called Grant Fleming from London; East London in fact, went to Paris to see The Jam, called it The Mod Pilgrimage, met loads of other Mods from London, came back and started a Mod scene. There's a tour of these Mod bands, Secret Affair and Purple Hearts, called March of The Mods, would love to go to that. I like Grant's take on Mod "Well Mod is a way of thinking, it's fun loving and smart. It was kids who wanted a laugh, drinking, dancing, girls. Going to gigs and taking pride in yourself". My mum typed it out for me at work, and it's on my wall, to act as a reminder. But he seems bored of Mod now, how can he be bored of Mod?

From the article, I see a lot of Mods come from East London and Essex, which most of my mother's family come from, even though she never likes to admit it. In fact we were there last Christmas at my grandparent's flat above a funeral parlour. My grandfather makes coffins for a living and gets the flat with the job, I like that as I often lay in the coffins like Count Dracula, much to the amusement of my grandparents, but not my actual parents. We take it in turns, sometimes my grandparents come to us, then the next year we go over there. They usually have more people and it's more of a party than just sitting round a table. In fact they like to play music, they play a lot of The Beatles as I told you and a lot of rock 'n' roll from the 50's, before Mod came out in the 60's. My uncle likes rock 'n' roll, I quite like it and often dance with him to Bill Hailey's Rock Around The Clock, he tells me he was a Teddy Boy, seen photos of him, he did look smart. There was a band a few years ago called Showaddywaddy saw loads on Top of The Pops who dressed like my uncle did, he tells me they don't know the first thing about being a Teddy Boy. I like this passion, I must have inherited his passion, because since discovering Mod it's become the most important thing in my life, I want to have all the clothes, see all the bands and I am reading whatever I can on it. Read an interview with Paul Weller the other day, first one, he's very clever and seems to be anti–society, I might learn to play the guitar and form a band.

Anyway enough of me rambling. Back to Christmas at my grandparents. It's late morning, all the adults are having a drink, us kids are playing with our toys or dancing, there's a loud knock on the front door, which is at the bottom of the stairs, so you have to walk down. My grandmother smiles and gets up to answer it, thinking it's an old friend coming to wish us all Merry Christmas and no doubt get a drink or two. Then I hear my grandmother angrily say "What do you want?" which isn't like her especially on Christmas Day

"Come on Eve, it's your brother Bill, just back from New Zealand". My word, my Uncle Bill, never met him, but my God heard his name enough times, he's the black sheep of the family. In the late sixties, I've been told over the years, he stole the social club's 'Christmas Club' money, not sure how much, but enough to go and live in Australia, no good byes or thanks. My mother tells me he had to leave Australia and go to live in New Zealand as he was involved in fixing local cricket matches and making a lot of money from bets, like it. The family talk about Bill a lot at Christmas, 'cos that's when he stole the money, suppose it reminds them. Heard he likes a drink and a punch up, never done an honest day's work in his life but always had money for wine, women and song, their words, not mine. As I said never met him until now. "I know who you bloody-well are, what do you want" never heard my grandmother so annoyed, "It's Christmas Day" pleads Bill "I know what day it is, thanks for telling me, goodbye". He must have put his foot in the door, heard the sound of it moving but not slamming.

"Please Eve, I've been finking,"

"That's a first".

"Please Eve, don't be cruel, I want to be with my family"

" Don't lie to me, knowing you, you've stolen some money from New Zealand, you thought you would come here, hoping we would forgive and forget, wrong Bill, we and the whole bleeding street went without our booze, presents and turkey, while you pissed off to Oz"

"I know, I am sorry, and I wanted to come back to see you, every day I know what I did was wrong".

My grandfather, who is usually calm and loves to spend Christmas Day in his comfortable chair with a bottle of beer, gets up and tosses his cherished beer bottle on the floor, shouts out as he is walking downstairs towards the front door

"Bill on the cobbles now",

"Alright Ernie, the cobbles it is"

Bill seems happy to fight my grandfather, this is better than the Christmas Carol Service on BBC.

Next thing, all of us, and the whole street are out in the road, with my grandfather and Bill facing each other, jackets off and their sleeves rolled up. My grandmother has gone upstairs with my mother to make some bacon sandwiches, she makes great bacon sandwiches. When my mother makes bacon sandwiches and often asks me if they are as good as my grandmother's, I have to lie and say yes, but they are not. All the crowd make a natural circle, bit like a boxing ring, my grandfather loves Henry Cooper. My parents tell me they used to see him around Soho. My grandfather and Bill face each other, my uncle steps in, talks to both of them and asking for a clean fight, just like the referee in boxing.

43

He steps back and the fighting starts, everyone is on my grandfather's side, oh yea I am as well, all I hear is

"Go on Ernie,"

"Chin him Ernie",

"Jab, hook, upper cut"

It's a good fight, and it is clear that Bill can box too, like a proper match; they break and have a drink, not sure if boxers drink beer and eat bacon sandwiches during their rests, but Bill and my grandfather do. The whole street is excited; me, my brother and my cousins are loving it. It lasts some time before my grandfather, like Henry Cooper, lands a punch that knocks Bill to the floor. My uncle goes over, counts to ten and pulls my grandfather's arm in the air, he's won by a KO and the whole street celebrates.

The next thing Bill is sitting with the whole family at the Christmas table, having lunch with us, joking with my grandmother and grandfather, it's like nothing has happened, and the fight has settled this bad feeling. If it had been at school it would have been the usual stand on the hall stage whilst Mrs Titchener goes on and on and on. This way it's dealt with and they move on, a much better way of doing things. Bill is now the centre of attention, I can't believe this, usually it's us, the younger children. Then, after lunch, my uncle starts to play his records again and everyone starts dancing. My grandmother and aunts, even my mother starts saying what a good dancer Bill was at dance halls in the 50s and 60s, we all stop dancing and let Bill do his stuff. He is good, like the way he moves, he is really good, I am watching, hopefully can remember his moves. He looks at me, winks then he seems to have trouble breathing, he's panting, he clutches his heart and collapses on the floor. My uncle runs over, looks for a heartbeat, feels his pulse, seen that loads of time on television, he looks at all of us and says "he's dead".

This is the best Christmas I have ever had.

V

A Roasting

I hate it when the summer holidays come to an end because all the bloody shops have posters reminding us that it's back to school soon, photos of happy parents and bleeding keen kids in their brand spanking new school clothes. If I was a child model I would refuse to do it, you're siding with the adults. What fucking kid is happy to go back to school, and as for school I am starting a new one, Rydens.

I wanted to go to Sunbury Comprehensive but my mother says she doesn't want me cycling on the busy road to Sunbury, her and her bloody busy roads, doesn't she understand I want to see my friends. Yet my father told me I would soon make new friends and my brother told me that Jimmy Pursey from Sham 69 went to Rydens - that's good. Talking of Sham 69, when I came back from the interview at the school, we drove past where the photo was taken for their single, Hersham Boys. I like that, so every day when I leave school I will cycle past the cover of a top ten single from a brilliant band, which is more than you can say about Sunbury. Maybe there are loads of Mods my age at Rydens. We could even form a band, read that The Jam was formed at school from lunch time music sessions. Going to learn to play the guitar, but can't ask for one yet as my mother bought me loads of clothes and she reminded me this morning that we will have to go clothes shopping again, but this time for school clothes. I tell you something, I ain't going to be one of those smiling kids happy to go back to school, bugger that.

Anyway school is about a month away and with my bike still under lock and key, and my friends from Sunbury are never in when I phone, not one of them has been bothered to cycle over to see me. I was hoping Peter would, but feel odd being a child calling an older boy and my mother said it wouldn't be a good idea. So I am spending my days watching TV, reading, becoming a real expert on Mod, and something called Two Tone, loads of good bands, Madness, The Beat, Specials, apparently based on music from the sixties called SKA, which I saw on All Mod Cons inner sleeve. Seen these bands on Tops of The Pops, and my brother has bought a few singles, Madness' The Prince and One Step Beyond, like the way they dress very Mod and they have a dancer called Chas Smash, he looks mad and fun. Like The Beat, have a single called Tears of a Clown, look like Mods, Specials are OK, but I find them a bit boring, their lead singer Terry Hall seems so miserable. But it's not just Mods who like them, but Skinheads, they look scary, no hair, green jackets, believe they're called flight jackets, big Doctor Martin boots, Levis jeans up to their ankles and Rude Boys, who wear black Harrington's, Fred Perry's and Sta Press, with small hats, Pork Pies, I think Kojak used to wear one. But they look like kids who can't make up their mind whether to be Skinheads or Mods. The Harrington's have loads of patches on them, and if they take them off they will look like normal kids. I want to look a Mod all the time even in bed, asked my mother for some Jam underpants, she told me they don't exist. Might write a letter to Paul Weller asking him to get some made, sure he will like the idea.

Been to Walton a few times, spoken some more times to the teenagers who work at Tower Records, they are the only people, apart from my family, I talk to. I bought another single the other day, Buzzcocks Harmony in My Head, love it, angry and loud, relate to the song. I haven't seen the dark haired boy who stole the chocolate bars, seen a few more older Mods, waved at them, but either they are annoyed or laugh at me. OK I may be a child, but I am still a Mod, I am wearing Tonic trousers, button down shirt or a Jam tee shirt and my Hush Puppy copies. Why can't they talk to me, what harm would it do? But only yesterday I did see two boys my age, well I think they are my age, one blonde and one dark hair on their bikes coming towards me, and the closer they got the more I could see they were Mods, the blonde haired boy just looked at me, whilst the dark haired boy faintly smiled. I smiled back as they rode past. Maybe I will meet them at the new school, it would have been nice if they had stopped and talked to me. It's another sunny day so I am going to walk into Walton after lunch. My mother leaves me a nice salad most days, or allows me to have some bread and cheese with one packet of crisps, she hides the rest. I have spent all day searching for them, all day. I think she takes them to work with her. So I have to make do with toast, but she does leave a bit of money, so today I am going to buy a nice ice cream and maybe walk towards the river.

My father told me many times, "variety is the spice of life", meaning try different things, so I will get my ice cream from a different newsagent. My mother told me off a long time ago for calling them sweet shops, as they sell newspapers mainly and sweets are just there to shut up the kids, apparently. There's a newsagent down one road, New Zealand Avenue, opposite the local police station. My brother had told me Monty Python used to film there. Like Monty Python, they are mad, bet Chas Smash from Madness is a fan. Sham 69, Psychomania and now Monty Python, music, films and comedy, all from my new town, good, very good. Anyway I want an ice cream, it will have to be an ice lolly, as can't find the Cornettos I have when I am on holiday in Italy, just walked in and I don't believe it, it's the fat red faced man who chased me and my 'new' friend. That was weeks ago, surely he won't recognise me, it didn't make Police 5, besides all he saw was the back of my head and I am smarter looking now. Anyway better I get my lolly, pay for it and go, they have got the Funny Feet ones, nice ice cream and the closest I can get to Italian ice cream. I give him my sweet smile, but he doesn't smile back, he remembers me but he just can't put his finger on it. I slowly put 10 pence on the counter, he takes the money and I slowly step back, just a couple more steps and I will be free, but alas no "You little shit, come here!"

I drop the ice cream and make a dash for it. I feel like I am in Grange Hill, and would you believe it, I crash into an adult, not just any adult but a tall ginger haired policeman, with the face of a Nazi prison guard, watched loads of films about the British escaping from prison of war camps. "PC McDonald, stop that thief!" I must have made the policeman's day, as he puts my arm behind my back, punches me in the stomach, and then marches me over the road to the police station. I am far too small and weak to fight back. Within about five minutes, I am sitting in a drab waiting room, one desk, one chair, a wooden bench and yellow walls, a few policemen come into the room and all say the same thing "You're for the high jump laddie." I'm scared, I wish I had gone to Knight's the newsagent, that's over the other side of the High Street. However, my father and my brother always told me if I was ever arrested to say nothing until either they or my mother arrives, not sure if they had experience of being arrested or just thought it would be a question of time before I was, perhaps both. Hard to keep calm.....

I can hear the shopkeeper in the reception area, "Please let me give him a punch, in the stomach, like you did, leave no marks". Oh fuck. "All in good time, first we need to interview him, and charge him." It's the ginger one. Just remember what your father and brother told you and think of all those episodes of The Sweeney, Kojak and Dixon of Dock Green you've watched, where the prisoner says nothing. MacDonald, with a real horrible smile, enters the room, sits down, looks at me for a minute, opens his nasty mouth "Come on son, confess now, I will put in a good word for you in Court. It's cauliflower cheese tonight at Feltham for tea, I hope you like that, because that's where you are going."

Oh my God, I am spending tonight at Borstal, no, what for, yes what for, and there won't be a break out, I didn't steal anything,

I didn't do it, I DIDN'T DO IT. I freeze unable to speak. Then a more senior policeman pokes his head round the door, he has more stripes down the side of his shirt. "You know you can't interview him, without his parents, you have to notify them." I smile at Ginger, he snarls back. But I do fear the wrath of my parents, perhaps a night in Feltham would have been the better option.

My father and mother have come to the station, she's in tears, but thank God for my father, as he points out I was arrested with no chocolate bars and I didn't know who the other boy was, therefore no evidence. The police hate him, but I love him, and have just been told they are going to let me go soon with no charge. However tonight's dinner won't be fun as my mother will tell me how ashamed she is. I have to be honest, I was scared at first, but now I can start my school telling my new class mates I've been arrested, surely every good Mod gets arrested every now and then. But I bet that ginger copper has his eye on me.

My first term at Rydens has been rather dull, after reading, hearing and seeing so much about Mod during the summer, I thought the whole school would be Mod. There are just two Mods in my year, Christopher Arnold and Simon Mott. No sign of the two young Mods I saw the other day or the dark haired boy who stole the chocolates. Arnold and Mott don't really talk to me.

The Jam brought out their fourth LP Setting Sons, and Secret Affair brought out their debut LP, Glory Boys, in November. I've listened to both LP's over and over. So pleased I have an older brother who buys these records as my mother or father surely wouldn't give me the money. But I have started a paper round, to save money and make friends. I will have money soon to buy some new clothes, but the other paper boys and girls all seem to know each other and don't really talk to me. Fuck them, they are not Mods, "faceless clowns" as Ian Page from Secret Affair would say. Read the sleeve notes of Glory Boys, I must say I like Ian Page's words, he writes them and Dave Cairns the guitarist writes the music. Like his playing, like the way they make Mod dark and moody like Batman, they dress very smart. Read a few interviews with Ian Page, love what he said about Mod to the NME "If punk was a question then mod is an answer - and some people don't like the answer!" Also love Secret Affair's take on Mod, Glory Boys, a better class of Mod, in smart trench coats and suits, no jeans or Fred Perry's, no badges or patches, Ian Page like Paul Weller is very intelligent.

Oh yea, got a parka, OK it's a Millet's one, but I am saving, as I said, to get a proper one, and my mother will give me the rest. Anyway took my patches and badges off after I found out about Glory Boys. Saw Mott with a nice cream Harrington on the other day with a Glory Boy badge, I went up to him and said "Love Glory Boys, favourite song is I'm Not Free but I'm Cheap ", he said it is a good song and walked off, how rude, all I wanted to do was talk. Arnold is in the same class as me, but we were graded straight away for Maths, English and French. I was put into the bottom set in all three, and he into the top, but I see him in History, Art, TD, Geography and other shit lessons. We have spoken a few times he's friendlier, and really likes Jam's Setting Sons. I like Setting Sons, read it was going to be an LP about three friends joining the army and their lives, but Weller didn't finish all the songs. They released a single from it, called Eton Rifles, about some un-employed working class kids marching past the school, Eton, and being jeered by the kids at that school, so they had a fight, wished I had been there. It made the Top Ten, first time for The Jam, I was so proud, and they were magic on Top of The Pops. Weller in this smart blue suit and a lovely scarf, Foxton looked good in a blue jacket and grey trousers, briefly saw his shoes, black with white stripes down the front, must get a pair and Buckler looked a real English gentleman in a boating blazer and straw hat.

They had four older teenagers dressed like Chelsea pension-ers by the side of Weller singing along to the chorus, they looked tough, might be their body guards. Best thing I have seen on Top of The Pops. Secret Affair have been on twice, Time for Action and Let Your Heart Dance, a real good song to dance to. As I said earlier Page and Cairns write the songs together, not like Weller who writes them on his own. But he always looks in a bad mood, so I bet Foxton and Buckler are too scared to join in.

I am not totally friendless, get on well with Ryden's 'rough boys', who all seem to like Two Tone more than Mod music. I haven't told anyone about being arrested, don't think they would believe me. There are some very pretty girls in my year, who are nice to me, but they all fancy Christopher Arnold, as he is very good looking. I don't play football with the rough boys as they are far too good for me, but we talk and have fun, they like me as I like to muck about. Briefly joined the Dungeons and Dragons club as I loved The Hobbit but the kids were mean to me. I lasted one session before I was killed off by a kid playing as an insane wizard, Leslie Stiles, that's his name, a bleeding girl's name, I will remember that Leslie. As I walked out of the room all I could hear was the laughter behind me. My mother and father keep telling me give it time as I am new there, and will make friends. I will be there for four years, four years, that sounds like a prison sentence.

I was expecting all the teasing about being Italian at Rydens, but there are a lot of Italians there, and a few black kids, never saw a black kid at Nursery Road. There is a pair of black twins, one of them appeared on the Sham 69's Hersham Boys single, I said hello to both of them one said "What are you looking at" and the other smiled, so I avoid them now. One of the Milky Bar Kids goes to Rydens, and he's in my year but he doesn't like to talk about it, so I have no idea what happened there. There are a few older Mods in the years above, some I had seen round Walton during the summer, one did walk past me, smile and say "We are The Mods", that made me happy. There are a few Skinheads, one booted me up the backside the other day in the dinner queue, and his friends laughed, so I try to avoid him as well as the black twins, well one of them. Evenings are the same as it's winter. I read, listen to music and watch TV, and you guessed it, my mother won't let me out on my bike in the dark. I've started reading thrillers as well as my Batman and Spiderman comics. I wonder if Ian Page reads comics. I cut out a photo of Page the other day so the next time I am going to get my hair cut I will show it to the barber and ask him to cut my hair like that.

Well Christmas was good, thought it might be bleak after the 'tragic' death of Uncle Bill, we didn't invite anyone over, but it was nice, good food and the BBC showed all The Beatles films over Christmas, loved them, really taking to John Lennon, he's funny and very clever. I got a brand new Tonic suit for Christmas, told you I would get a present, I knew I would. My brother bought me two Soul Music Compilation LPs, all music from the sixties, two record labels, never heard of them before, Stax and Motown, but there again never really thought about record labels before until this Christmas, now want to know which bands are with which record labels, not going to list who is with who, that will bore ya. My brother told me that the original Mods in the sixties liked soul music a lot, at first I was annoyed with his present, but after I played them I like them, no I love them. Pleased my brother is helping me in becoming a better Mod, in fact my whole family is, think they are happy I have interest outside of horror films, comics and football.

One of the albums has a song called Going to a Go Go, by Smokey Robinson which Secret Affair did a version of, that's called a cover version. Now I can see the connection between Soul and Mod. Soul music is music made by black Americans, it's upbeat, a real honest sound to it, the voices are wonderful, as is the music, not angry or loud, makes me feel good and happy, great to dance to, but I am not allowed to dance to it in my new suit, as my mother says it will crease it. Also heard a song called Midnight Hour by Wilson Pickett which was covered by The Jam, but their version is much harsher. That's what I love about Mod, I am learning new and exciting things all the time. And life at Rydens just gets better.

I was expecting another term of speaking to people but having no real friends, then Christopher made a point of sitting next to me at the morning registration "Nice Christmas? See you're still a Mod. Mott and me thought you were a poser and become a Rude Boy after Christmas." Oh so they were watching me, now they can see I am a real Mod "Well I thought you and Mott were Rude Boys" I replied. Christopher laughed, then chatted about presents, told him about my new suit and Soul LPS, he got loads more than me, then he invited me to his house for lunch which is about a 2 minute walk from the school, said he can get some chips from the Halfway, that's a parade of shops near our school, and take them back to his place. But Ryden's don't allow 1st year's out during lunch and my mother told me to stay at school during lunch, so I could only say yes, as breaking the rules is good fun and it's been a long time.

Sneaking out for chips was brilliant, like The Great Escape, they have some kid from the Sixth Form watching the gate, but he's too busy chatting up the girls, they dig it! Told you any chance to quote The Jam. Christopher seems really good fun, and his house is massive, three floors, could see Sherlock Holmes living here. His father works for Selfridges, his mother works for Harrods, so loads of lovely furniture and he has the whole top floor to himself - I would love that. We ate our chips in his big kitchen, my mother will like me being friends with him, listened to the radio and then he invites me to the local youth club this Friday, have heard the rough boys talk about it, but they never invited me. Christopher tells me there will be some Mods there our age, but from a nearby school, Heathside, I can't wait.

Friday couldn't come too soon. I cycled over to Christopher's, didn't want to go on my own as I still don't know that many people and Mott was there, he looked dead smart, white Sta Press, and a checked button down, with a trench coat with his Glory Boy badge. Whilst Christopher had a Polo neck on, just like The Beatles, with light blue Levis Jeans, both wearing Hush Puppies. Like the Polo neck look, first Mod I've seen with one on. My mother has a few Polo necks, lovely colours, she bought them when we were in Milan, going to have to borrow them. Me, got my new Tonic suit on, white Ben Sherman copy, Rustlers and sporting my new Ian Page haircut, the barber had done a good job and followed it well, even went on my own, first time, if my mother had been there she would have gone for the traditional short back and sides. Mott remarked how smart I looked, which I liked, but he did say I need a proper Parka or a better coat, so I left my parka at Christopher's, he's wearing his, but it's a proper one.

Walking there was brilliant, first time since I became a Mod I have been with other Mods for a day, an evening or whatever. We talked of course mainly about Mods, with Mott saying that Glory Boys is a 'true' Mod LP whilst Setting Sons is New Wave - I didn't agree. We also chatted about Madness and their LP One Step Beyond, which came out late last year, my brother also bought that this year. Listened to it a lot, one song I like is Razor Blade Alley, not their usual 'nutty sound', oh the nutty sound is what Madness call their music, which is a mix between SKA, Punk and Pop, Madness seem to be very popular with Skinheads.

Mott is very deep, but I like that. Like me, he listens to other music, he reckons that Joe Jackson, he's a singer who seems to sing jazz type songs, is a Mod sound. I said I thought that The Pretenders with their single, Brass in Pocket, and their singer, a beautiful woman called Chrissie Hyde had a new soul sound, Mott's eyes lit up when I said that, even though I had no idea what it meant, just something I read in NME or Melody Maker I think, but he could tell I took my music seriously. Mott told me to watch for a band called Dexy's Midnight Runners if I like soul, I have taken note, seen the name yet to hear their music.

The youth club is down a road called Crutchfield Lane. Believe it or not it's called Crutchfield Lane Youth Club, but everyone just calls it Crutchfield. It's near a church named St Andrew's and the Vicar runs the youth club. I was told by Christopher and Mott when I hear the opening bit of Madness' One Step Beyond that I am not to dance as the Vicar likes to have a dance, I just chuckled as I thought they were joking and I was being fooled.

When I got there, I was surprised to see so many familiar faces from school, most wearing Harrington's and dressing like Rude Boys. In the court yard and behind there is this old building, guess that is the youth club, these kids don't dress like Rude Boys at school. You can't be a part time Rude Boy, just like you can't be a part time Mod, anyway they all say hello, and a few say how much they like my suit, they are a good bunch of lads, shame they aren't Mods though. There are a lot of girls from my year there too, all smiling at Christopher, even some older girls come over and say how nice he looks, even to Mott, but not to me, apart from one girl, Susie I think she is called, she's in another class, she smiles at me, I mean a genuine smile. I smile back and it seems to last forever, we are just looking at each other smiling, it's a magical feeling then the spell is broken when a friend calls her over, she looks over her shoulder smiling as she walks off - she is beautiful. I mouth the words bye and she does the same, it must be this suit and my hair cut. I have never felt like this before, my word, I love it.

There's a few kids in baggy jeans with orange stripes down the side, hanging about the court yard. They have long hair on top that goes to the side, bright coloured tee shirts, in fact one of the black twins, the moody one is one of them. He gives me a snarl, I look away, fuck this, one minute I'm smiling at a beautiful girl, then I am avoiding Rydens answer to Muhammad Ali. Mott tells me they are called Soul Boys, not sixties soul, but something called jazz funk. I hate to say it, and I dare not say it in front of my new friends, that they look smart in an odd way, a nice uniform and they look quite tough. No Punks here tonight, seen a few at Rydens, not many, only one in my year, David Bold. He is mad and he did have me in a headlock the other day telling me he eats Mods for breakfast, but somehow I could tell he was joking, got a feeling me and him will become friends.

A black boy in my class, call Rashid, is also here tonight, dressed as a Rude Boy, the smartest one, as he has a black suit on, just like The Jam from In The City, black shirt, white tie and a Pork Pie hat. Seen the one he's got on at Badges, Bits and Bobs and just one badge, The Specials. Rash, we call him, told me Bold is the toughest in our year, but won't hit anyone and confirmed he likes to play hard with us, so I can expect a few more headlocks. In fact

Rash comes over and shakes my hand, shakes my hand, I like his style, nice manners, he's smoking a cigarette, moving his head, he seems natural, excited and happy. We get on well at school, didn't at first, but we became mates after we had a bundle. I said in the English class, we are both in the bottom group, that The Jam were better than The Specials, he followed me outside and tried to give me a dead leg, so we wrestled and fell into a bush, with the rest of the class laughing only to be pulled up by another evil PS Teacher, Mr Hare, looks like and thinks he's Bodie from The Professionals. What is it about PE teachers, they just love to push kids around. Rash and I didn't tell on each other, said we both fell over at the same time, Hare or Hartley Hare as we call him, let us go, but Rash did give me a dead arm as he walked off, and I shouted out "The Specials are shit", he just turned round gave me two fingers with a beaming smile and a wink, from that day, we became mates.

Then I see the boy who stole the chocolate, and he's a Mod now, dressed quite basic, blue Tonic trousers, red Fred Perry, bit of a colour clash, with a Parka but he has black suede boots on, like those a lot. Even though I am not an expert, looks like he only converted to Mod the other week and this is his first outfit. Then I can't believe my luck, the dark haired and blonde haired boys, who I saw on their bikes the other day are here. The dark haired one looks good, a real nice blue button down shirt and smart blue trousers, not Tonics or Sta Press, and a black type mac, with a Union Jack badge, and the blonde haired one is also smart, boating blazer, white Sta Press, and he's got white type plimsolls on, both well-dressed Mods. At last I have found some other Mod friends. I walk straight up to the Italian looking boy "Remember me".

"Yes April's Fool's Day 1975, you fell in dog's poo" his quirky reply, the others start laughing, I have no choice but to join in, in fact we don't say anything for about five minutes, just laughing, he stops then starts laughing again, he's not serious like Mott, I break the hilarity "So you became a Mod", he raises one eye brow, "Oh yes".

"Are you Italian?"

"Italian ha," again he starts to laugh hysterically, so it starts all over again, with others joining in, with him muttering " Italian, please," then he wipes a tear of laughter from his eye " No, Greek".

"Greek", I start laughing hoping to get it going again, but he looks at me seriously, as do the blonde kid and the other dark haired kid "What's so funny about that?"

"Well what's so funny about being Italian?"

Everything", he starts laughing and the others join in, I have no idea how long this madness will last.

Eventually, after the laughter stops, we chat in the court yard for a long time, I find out his name is Vincent Anastopoulos, but he calls himself Vinnie, originally from East London, moved to Weybridge, near Walton, in 1974. His father is half Greek and from North London, and his mother is from East London, his father bought a restaurant down here and brought the family down. The blonde haired one is Tom Ryan, not sure where he's originally from and the other dark haired one is Richard James, but after becoming a Mod, calls himself Rick, as in Rick Buckler from The Jam, well that's what Vinnie told me. Christopher and Mott come over, and Christopher tells me these are Mods from Heathside School, so happy to meet them. We go into the main building's entrance by the side of the stairs and pay our ten pence to get in. Mott tells me there is a pool room and a tuck shop up-stairs, got fifty pence, so will get a can of coke and some crisps, and some chips on the way home.

After practising dancing on my own for a long time, I can't wait to show the world my real moves. The music playing sounds disco, remember that from the discos at Nursery Road, but with more attitude, this must be jazz funk, it's good, I like it. The soul boys are dancing to it with real passion, this is amazing to watch, they are so serious, never seen this before, they move about, shake their hips, I want to join in, I can feel the music, I can really feel it. Some of the older girls are also dancing, they are gorgeous and they have the same passion as the soul boys. The 'evil' black twin is dancing and catches me watching, he gives me a wink, a wink, thank God for that, must have seen me talking to Rash, now I am really happy.

Then I hear

Hey you, don't watch that, Watch this! This is the heavy heavy monster sound, The nuttiest sound around, So if you've come in off the street, And you're beginning to feel the heat, Well listen buster, You better start to move your feet To the rockiest, rock-steady beat, Of Madness, One step beyond!"

The soul boys and girls leave the dance floor and walk straight out. I move forward to dance, thinking it was a fib about the vicar but Mott pulls me back and shakes his head as if to say no, then this bearded and chubby Vicar, wearing the dog collar and all that, walks from the behind a desk with two record players on it, all the kids move to the side allowing him space and the moment the opening saxophone kicks he starts to dance just like Chas Smash and Suggs from Madness. I look at all the kid's faces, no one not even Vinnie is laughing, I can't believe what I am seeing, a Vicar dancing like a lunatic to Madness, and no one apart from me finds this funny.

VI

Just a Cheese Sandwich

After the 'groovy Vicar' had finished we were allowed to dance. The first time, well apart from at my grandparents at Christmas, I've danced in public. I did try and dance at a school disco at Nursery Road Middle School once, but the girls, even some of the boys and a few teachers all stopped and laughed at me. But they couldn't now, no way, I was way too good. I was at one with the music, the 'groovy Vicar' starts playing Two Tone and Mod music, the Soul boys and girls have left Crutchfield all together. Christopher tells me they come before they go to The Hop. That's a disco in a hall in Walton for older teenagers, only plays disco, jazz funk - no Mod music or that's what Christopher's sister says to him. Perhaps she doesn't want him and his friends to go.

The 'groovy' Vicar has all the songs and when he plays Secret Affair's *Let Your Heart Dance*, I go mad, but in time to the music and the line "Dancing to the teenager ideal" touches my heart. Ian Page is sussed, learnt that word the other day after listening to Secret Affair's *Soho Strut*, it means you know what is going on.

Here I am, I've just turned a teenager and only became a Mod last year, yet it seems to make so much sense, like it was meant to be. I am looking smart, so are my new friends, we are all dancing to our music, our hymns, our anthems, in fact we take over the floor.

The other kids all look on, some are even dancing, like Rash; he is a natural, moves in time with his massive beaming smile.

I like him and dance with him to The Beat's *Tears of a Clown* and The Special's *Gangsters*. Been a bit unfair on Two Tone, reading about it, like the way they want to unite black and white kids, went through so many years in Sunbury of racism, why, 'cos I am half Italian - so what? I like the concept on unity, like that a lot, like me and Rash being mates, now that would be unheard of in Sunbury, and God forbid if a black man had moved into Ravendale Road. Bet Mr Bates would have formed their answer to the Klu Klux Klan, what a bastard he was. Then the 'groovy Vicar' goes back to Mod and plays The Jam's *When You're Young*, Tom breaks away from everyone, I follow him, it's just me and him, singing along to Woaaahhh. This is our song, the words are for us, The Jam recorded this one for us.

Tom, like me, knows all the words, he smiles, I smile back, the song breaks down, I think that's called a middle eight, then when it builds up I do a 'Jam' jump. Weller or Foxton jump as high as they can with their guitar or bass whilst pulling their legs behind their backs, seen some good photos. I have been practising this for ages in my bedroom, got the bruises to prove it. But tonight I am perfect. Tom nods his head in appreciation, so do Christopher, Rick and Mott. I look at Vinnie and with his right index finger he circles round his head as if to say I am mad, me mad? He's the one that steals chocolate bars for a laugh. But the Groovy Vicar clears the dance floor, when he decides to 'spin' (learnt that word too, means to play a record, not sure where from though) The Merton Parkas *You Need Wheels*. I heard this last summer; apparently it was the first Mod revival or renewal single. I found it dull then and I still find it dull now, as do all the other kids. So I decide to go upstairs and buy a coke and some crisps, don't bother asking the others, I feel comfortable and secure knowing that they are here. On the way up to the tuck shop, some of my 'new school mates' say hello, I say hello back. I feel I have finally arrived at Rydens and been accepted by the Mods, I couldn't be happier.

Pay my money for a can of coke and cheese and onion crisps, count my change, I have enough for a bag of chips on the way home. I do like chips, but couldn't eat them all the time; I am feeling on top of the world. 'Top of the World Ma', heard that in a James Cagney film, White Heat, my father loves him and I watched it with him as BBC showed a few of them over Christmas a few years back, Cagney and Humphrey Bogart always playing gangsters. Both 'cool' men, who look good in suits, sadly for them they were born before Mod and in the wrong country, as I don't think the Yanks, have Mods.

Rash told me to go to the pool room opposite the tuck shop for a game, never played before, but sure it will be fun. This is a big mistake, I walk in and standing there before me are three Skinheads, two of them playing pool but they all stop to look at me. I hadn't noticed them come in, I've seen them at Rydens, a few years above me, one of them is the one that kicked me up the backside, two of them are dressed very smart in long black overcoats, called Crombies and smart dark leather shoes, with tassels, called loafers, wouldn't mind a pair in black without the tassels, seen them in Jack Brendon's. Both are wearing grey Sta Press, the other one, the one who kicked me up the arse, is wearing a denim jacket, tight jeans all bleached with ox blood Doctor Martin boots, no Mod would be seen in them. He's the biggest and seems to be the leader. With them are four girls, about 16 or 17, trying to look like Farrah Fawcett or Jaclyn Smith's from Charlie's Angels but looking more like Cathy Hargreaves or Trisha Yates from Grange Hill. But I could see them quite easily posing in The Sun's Page Three, in fact one of the girls smiles at me, the other three don't and three Skinheads look on at me menacingly. I freeze and look at the main Skinhead, put my head down look straight at his boots and the bright red shoe laces. Christopher told me that Skinhead's shoes laces have a code, and red I think, means you are a poof, but I am not sure if Christopher was teasing me. "What the fuck are you looking at, you plastic Mod" snaps the brutal Skinhead.

"Leave him alone Paul, he's only a kid" pleads the only girl that smiled at me.

Shut it Sam or you'll get my right hand across your face."

"Like to see you try" - she yells.

He's annoyed that she has answered him back; he seems confused whether to hit me or Sam. I have no idea why, but I say "I'm looking at your laces", the moment the words came out of my mouth, I think what have I said?

"Hit him Paul, he's being cheeky" butts in one of the smartly dressed Skinheads. He doesn't hit me but grabs both lapels of my jacket, pulls me off the ground and pushes me against the wall. "Maybe I'll bum ya first, then give you a good leathering".

I start to tremble; he sees my fear and loves it.

"Where did you get your suit? Off one of Ken Dodd's Diddy Men", all his friends, well the men do, laugh. Sam, and now her friends, don't look impressed.

"Please, I haven't done anything" I plead, hoping that he might let me go.

"Please, you cunt, please ha", then my prayers are answered.

"Pemberton, picking on fucking kids again, you fucking cock!"

The Skinhead, who must be called Paul Pemberton, let's go of me. I drop to the ground, turn my head to the entrance, and see two older well-dressed Mods in suits, one dark brown, one blue, like Weller's when he did Eton Rifles on Top of The Pops, both wearing green trench coats, opened so you can see the suits. I look down at their footwear, they must have been to Jack Brendon's they are both wearing tassel free black loafers, no badges, no patches. They must be Glory Boys, they look so smart, in fact seen them in Walton before, but by then I have given up saying hello to older Mods, got bored of being annoyed or laughed at.

Pemberton looks scared of these two and says "Just having a laugh Snowy." Snowy, why Snowy, then I see his hair, it's all white, he must only be 17 or 18, Pemberton looks at me, nods his head winks and pulls me up, I move back out of his reach and say "No, he wanted to bum me and beat me up…. Snowy". Snowy looks a bit taken back that I had called him by his name. The silent Mod, a little bit smaller moves towards the thug.

"You fucking little toe rag!" screams Pemberton, and he hits me on the jaw, I fall on the floor and I can see his DM boot about to come crashing into my head, then I heard a loud thud both his legs drop horizontally. I look up and see Snowy standing over him with two clenched fists; he's knocked the bully out. The silent Mod moves into the other two, one runs for it and the other is trapped, the silent Mod starts to punch him in the face and the stomach, the Skinhead can't even put up a fight, the girls are screaming. Snowy tells them to shut up and helps me up "Nice suit" he says, "Not as nice as yours" I reply, he smiles.

Pemberton starts to get up slowly with his right arm whilst holding his left arm up above his face, as if to say I surrender, he catches my gaze, I smile, a big smile. I've been rescued by the Glory Boys. "Martin" I hear an adult voice. - It's the groovy Vicar "Paul". I bet the Skinhead that ran away went and told the Vicar, what a baby. Martin must be Snowy, the Vicar looks at the silent Mod, who says nothings just pulls out a packet of cigarettes, takes one out and lights it, the vicar turns back to Snowy and Pemberton, who are now like naughty school children. Snowy and Pemberton stand side by side, bow their heads and say sorry. My word this groovy Vicar really runs the place, no one can dance when he does and he can stop a fight. He looks at me, "Go downstairs and enjoy the rest of the night, I want to talk to this lot …. Alone" I am happy to oblige and as I walk out both Snowy and even the silent Mod smile at me - that was exciting

I came down to a hero's reception, as word had got out quickly. Vinnie seems genuinely concerned and eager for action, the others are too. But it's Vinnie who wants to fight the Skinheads. We talk for about 10 minutes or so, then there's a slight tap on my shoulder, its Snowy - "You alright mate?"

"Yes."

"Have a fag mate to calm down."

I had never smoked in my life before, but Weller always looks good with a cigarette, so I take one, reckon my mother would go mad if she knew this. Don't know what brand it is, it makes me cough, but it's my first cigarette. There's a bit of laughter due to me coughing, then the silent Mod suddenly speaks - "You're too young to smoke."

Snowy chuckles as we all do and he turns his attention to my new Mod friends.

"You fuckers ran, your mate was in trouble, none of you helped him out. Mods stick together."

All of them put their heads down in shame, and then Vinnie looks up and says "we didn't know where he was." Snowy gives him a clout round the head.

"Shut up and don't speak when I am talking to you." Vinnie looks annoyed, maybe if he was two inches taller and a stone or so heavier he would fight back, I can see the anger in his eyes. I decide to stick up for Vinnie - "Snowy, they didn't know I was in trouble, I went upstairs on my own". Snowy looks at them and me, "OK, but you need to look out for each other, Skinheads and other cunts like that will pick you out if you're on your own. Like I said Mods stick together."

Vinnie and I exchanged firm glances, as if to say, we will. Then the silent Mod speaks again, so he ain't really the silent Mod anymore - "Come on Snowy, we need to catch the train for London, you said you were popping in here for a second to drop something off for your mother."

Snowy nods, and says good bye. "Where are you going? " I ask Snowy, but the (non) silent Mod replies "See The Chords," before I can ask if I can join them, he adds "No, you can't come, this is for Mods, not Puppy Mods", and laughs.

Snowy doesn't, in fact gives the (non) silent Mod a disapproving shake of his head. As they both walk off, Vinnie shouts "We are not fucking Puppy Mods, we are Mods, Mods." Vinnie's clothes might be basic, but he sure comes across brave and tough, got a feeling him and me are going to be good friends.

'Crutchfield' has certainly become the highlight of our week, been going there for a couple of months now and I love it, gives me a chance to dress up, wear all my Mod clothes. Not going into detail about my 'glad rags' all the time as it will bore you and I am sure you get the picture now that me and my friends are smart, 'sussed', and thanks to my mother's Italian cashmere and tennis shirts which fit me, I look good every Friday night. I was pleased to find out Tom and Rick live near me, not even a bike ride away, so Rick knocks for me on a Friday with Vinnie and we knock for Tom and walk to Crutchfield.

Vinnie lives in a big house, well it's a mansion on a private estate called Burwood Park, massive houses in woodlands, he cycles over and back to Rick's every Friday. Been to his house, biggest house I have ever been in, he invited us all over, all of us, Christopher, Mott, Tom, Rick and of course me. He has his own living room on the side of the house with a TV and a record player as well as bedroom with his own toilet - I want to move in. Next to Burwood Park is an even bigger private estate called St George's Hill, read that during the mid-sixties John Lennon and Ringo Starr lived there, whilst George Harrison lived nearby in Esher, made me very proud that I live near where three of The Beatles once lived. My brother told me anarchy was founded in St George's Hill, some peasant revolt many centuries ago, even better.

Vinnie still hates The Jam and the other bands, but likes soul music and of course The Beatles. Tom is a real expert on music, more advanced than me and Mott. He introduced me to another sixties band called The Small Faces, he has an LP by them, Small Faces Big Hits, love the music, like The Beatles meets soul music. Their lead singer, Steve Marriott, has a wonderful voice, unbelievable and they are better dressed than The Jam, Secret Affair and The Who. Tom even introduced me to a book called Mods! by Richard Barnes, about the original London Mods, loads of great photos and the story of how they lived, different names for Mods, like Seven and Six, means cheap and a Face means best Mod, Tom says he is a Face, so does Mott. I am not bothered about being a Face, just want to be a good Mod, to me that's more than enough.

He reads bits out to me, it's like a sermon in Church only this time it means something to me. He got the book in Badges, Bits and Bobs, I must have missed it or been looking at Batman comics instead. Next time I go to Kingston I will get a copy, as now I can go there on my own. Rick is an interesting Mod, different in terms of dress sense, dark colours that work. Even dyed his parka black and looks good. He likes to draw and he's good, an artist my mother calls him. My parents like my new friends, especially Vinnie. Forgot to say, at long last got a proper Parka, no badges or patches.

Started talking to Susie a lot more at Rydens and Crutchfield, in fact spent the whole lunch hour sitting with her on some steps, I do like her, but I am a bit shy to ask her out yet. Rash has come back to my house a few times after school - he's a laugh. I have to watch out for Pemberton at school, he leaves soon but I still avoid him, but when he does sees me just shakes his fist and shouts out "I am going to bum ya one day." Him and his obsession with my backside, it's not natural. I don't really hang about with Christopher and Mott much at school now, but more with the 'Rough' 'Rude' and 'Soul' boys, but I am going to call them 'the boys' from now on, makes it easier, as they do change their look from one week to the next.

But to be honest, most of the kids at school in all the years aren't really into fashion, in fact they look quite dull, I just like talking about and speaking to the ones that are, much more interesting. The boys like to tease the teachers, especially our Year Head Mr 'George' Young, otherwise known as Chicken George to us, he looks really old, wears a tweed jacket with grey scruffy hair and sensible comfortable shoes. We go outside his office door or underneath his window, cluck like a chicken, run off and hide. He usually comes out, followed by his Assistant Head, Mrs Vaughn, a small badly dressed woman, short pudding basin haircut with glasses, in fact she looks like Velma from Scooby Doo. Wears a skirt, with socks pulled right up to her knees and I am telling ya, you can see the hairs on her legs. She ain't no Victoria Principal, now there's a real woman for you. Every time she walks past us, Mrs Vaughn that is, not Victoria Principal, we sing "Scooby Dooby Doo, where are you, We've got some work to do now, Scooby Dooby Doo, where are you, We need some help from you now," she tells us to shut up, just like Windsor Davies from It Ain't Half Hot Mum, but she doesn't know it's all about her, which makes it even funnier.

Rydens School is not just one block but a main building with loads of other buildings, like the North, East, West and South blocks, two up and two down, but in this case two down and four up with one small office on the top for the Year Head. However Mr Young's office is by the side entrance in the main building, which is good for us as we have more escape options.

I heard these blocks were built when they increased the school leaving age from 15 to 16 eight years ago in 1972. They were meant to be temporary, but they ran out of money and so they have stayed. Can you imagine being 14 in 1970, thinking cushty I am leaving school next year, only to be told you've got another year, fuck that, seriously fuck that. Our history teacher, Miss Alderton, she's alright, nice to us, told me her older brother was an original Mod in the 60s, but she said they didn't do the 'youth culture' thing. I think she did, looking at photos from birds in the late 60's, she looked like she was a hippy, smoked dope and took LSD. Oh yeah reading up on The Beatles and the late 60's in general, got to know about these drugs. They do sound like fun, didn't at first when I first read about them. A few kids at school say their brothers or sisters smoke dope, pop pills, and have orgies, when I see it, I will believe it. Anyway, Miss Alderton said she was a student teacher in East London in 1971 and when the kids heard about the school leaving age they had a mini riot on their hands, mainly Skinheads, who came after the Mods in the sixties don't know if I told you that.

Talking of Skinheads, The Specials had a Number One a few weeks back *Too Much Too Young*, it's an EP, they have covered some classic SKA numbers *Guns of Navarone, Long Shot Kick De Bucket, The*

Liquidator and *Skinhead Moonstomp*. First time really listened to SKA
- like it a lot. Again like soul music, nice beat, comes from Jamaica
as soul comes from America. Rick likes SKA a lot and listens to the
modern version, Reggae, not my cup of tea, but I get it. Yet I just
like the sight and sound of well-dressed men playing their instru-
ments hard and well from the heart like The Jam or The Who or
a black Yank singing well and with passion like Otis Redding or
Wilson Pickett, never seen any real clips but loads of photos.

Got my first detention the other day, Rash, me and Mark Cross,
who wants to be a Skinhead, but his mother won't let have him
the haircut so he's a Rude Boy, always smiling and laughing. We
walked past Chicken George's office as we were leaving, stood
outside for a second, done the clucking sound and were about to
scarper, but as we turned round, he and Mrs Vaughn were standing behind us. I think they were hiding in the broom cupboard
opposite to catch us, as we had been doing the chicken sound
about four times a day now. He marched us straight back into his
office. After my run in with Ginger MacDonald this is nothing. He
sits down, with Mrs Vaughn standing behind him, can't believe
she is a Mrs, who the fuck would want to marry her? His words
seriously go over my head, again got used to this at Nursery Road
Middle School with Mrs Titchener, looking at Rash and Mark they
are used to it too.

At least he won't get us to stand on the stage in the main hall. As
he is going on about respect, discipline and disgrace and all that
shit. I look up and behind him is a life size portrait of The Queen,
never noticed that before, that surely needs a visit from me and
my marker pen - I have taken note.

After the lecture we are marched to the History Block which
is the West block to join the third year detention, as they didn't
know where the first and second year detentions were. Which was
good for me, Mark and Rash as Miss Alderton was taking it, only
five other kids doing detention when we got there. One of the
kids, an older Mod called Karl, don't know his surname, smart
and quite friendly, in fact he was the one who said to me We are

The Mods when I started Rydens, he smiles, nods and gives me a wink, I do the same, hopefully that will get back to the other older Mods, that I got into trouble. Miss Alderton lets us grab a history book each to read, whilst she carries on doing the crossword in her newspaper, she looks as bored and as pissed off as us. I read up on the failed gunpowder plot of 1605, whilst reading it I feel sad that they failed to blow out the Houses of Parliament.

The other night me and my brother were listening to The John Peel Show in his bedroom. John Peel is a DJ on Radio One at 10 p.m. at night, he plays all the bands, Mod, Punk, New Wave, Two Tone, Reggae, you name it and he gets copies of the singles before we can buy them, sounds like a good job. When he announced he was going to play The Jam's new single, my brother and I jumped for joy like it was Christmas morning. Talking of the festive season, my brother got a new stereo for Christmas, the old record player he has given to me and with his new one you can record an LP or single straight off the radio onto the tape machine. Peel announces The Jam's new song *Going Underground*, my brother hits the record button, the opening is quite military, hits you hard, powerful as only The Jam can do, with Weller coming in with - "Some people might say my life is in a rut," got so used to his voice, can make the words out straight away, give or take the misquote. Then the song builds and builds, and bang it's over in about three minutes, but what an amazing three minutes, I'm speechless. It's better than *Eton Rifles* and that was brilliant. Then we read in the NME that week they are going to have a free live EP, *Down At Tube Station at Midnight* and *Away From The Numbers* with the first 100,000 or 200,000 copies sold can't remember the exact number. The next day my brother goes down to Tower Records and pre-orders it.

The Jam went straight in at Number One. Number One, I couldn't believe it, so proud, we had done it, a gang of outsiders Number One, a fucking Mod band, top of the charts. Played the single over and over again, love the live songs on the EP, never heard The Jam live before, it's raw, lively, strong and of course full of passion, Buckler's drumming on Tube Station takes my breath away. Even though *Going Underground* is the main song, in fact it's a double A- side, meaning that there's no B-side, and the other A–side *Dreams of Children* was going to be the main song, with *Going Underground* being the B-side, there was a fuck up so they made both the A-side, "Confused? You won't be after this episode of "Soap," well I am, anyway *Dreams of Children* is like Punk meets the Beatles and I love the sharp lyrics "I caught a glimpse from the dreams of children. I got a feeling of optimism. But woke up to a grey and lonely picture." That's how I feel a lot of the time, it feels like Weller knows us, really knows us

First Top of The Pops appearance The Jam couldn't appear playing live as I think they were in America, so they played the video instead. Weller looked amazing in a paisley scarf, Foxton giving it his all and Buckler mean moody and magnificent, must get a paisley scarf, but I did say that to myself in November. My brother and I loved the video; even my father and mother said it was a good song. The next week they were Number One again, my father and mother had gone out and my brother had gone round to his girlfriend's house and, for some reason, I was happy to watch it on my own. I wasn't going to invite any friends round; I had become a fan on my own. OK, Peter, Mark and my brother helped me, but it was me on my own listening to their music over and over again, they became mine, a voice of reassurance and a window to the outside world and they still are.

I am so pleased I did watch it on my own, they looked like heroes, well they are heroes, playing a wonderful song. Weller with this Heinz Creamed Tomato Soup apron on, but wearing it inside out, love it, really love it, only he can make wearing an apron look good. Bruce and Rick look strong and commanding, then at one point Weller slightly gazes to the camera, like he's sharing the moment with all their fans, and saying to us "we done it, thank you." I break into tears, real tears, I have never been moved by an emotion like this before. Of course I have cried before due to being hurt but this was out of pride, we had done it, we really

70

had done it, fuck the teachers, fuck Rydens, fuck PC MacDonald, fuck Mr Bates, fuck the shop keeper, fuck Pemberton, The Jam are Number One.

After Top of The Pops I turn off the TV and sit in total silence, I am thinking and reliving what I have just seen, the greatest appearance ever on Top of The Pops. Then I start to wish my father had bought one of those video recorders; Christopher, Mott and Vinnie have got one, wondering whether they had recorded it and knowing full well it's pointless asking Vinnie as he hates The Jam. My mother and father came back around 10 p.m. and the first thing I say to my mother "Could you buy me a Heinz Creamed Tomato Soup apron please?"

"Do you need one for Home Economics class then?" she replies.

VII

All in A Good Day's

I know I would bore you no end if I told you what me and my mates had been up to day by day, week by week, month by month, so it's over a year ago since The Jam went to Number One, and their next single Start also got to Number One. It didn't go straight in as Going Underground did, but it got to top of the charts, made my summer. Sadly there was no Top of The Pops appearance, but they did show a brilliant video of the three of them in a room enclosed with all these shutters. Bruce was in a lovely burgundy box jacket with a Start tee-shirt, Paul in a black shirt, paisley tie and round glasses like John Lennon used to wear, and Rick looking very casual but cool in a light blue button down. Paul playing this guitar with an amazing paint job, an explosion with the words Whaam! Just like The Batman TV show. My brother says it's called Pop Art, apparently trendy art from the sixties, and he said it started in the late 50s where they made art out of adverts and comics, like it and the name…. Pop Art!

Two years since becoming Mod neither Rick, Tom or me wear the standard uniform of 1979; we are pretty individual in terms of clothes. Vinnie still dresses in the traditional sense though, Sta Press, Fred Perry tennis shirt and jumpers, that sort of thing, he still looks smart. During the summer holiday Christopher stopped being a Mod. Couldn't believe it, to me you are a Mod for life. I thought he was a traitor at first but he still likes a laugh, so it's hard to hate him and my mother said I shouldn't dislike someone 'cos they dress different to you.

I don't really talk that much to Mott; he still comes out for the big occasions, but not for the mucking about, riding bikes and annoying people. So Vinnie, Tom and Rick have become my best friends, all for different reasons. Vinnie it's the laughter, madness, mayhem, mischief and with Tom and Rick it's about the clothes, attitude and the music. Tom likes all the Mod stuff, sixties bands and soul and today's music whilst Rick goes beyond that, he likes a lot of reggae, as I told ya, and funk music, he has an older brother who plays bass, with a great record collection.

I like going round Rick's, always plays me different records which I like and Mods are meant to like, but I am not bothered. Rick looks Mod but doesn't look Mod, if that makes sense. Oh yea, when Mott told me to look out for Dexy's Midnight Runners he wasn't wrong, loved their album Searching for Young Soul Rebels, bought it from Tower Records, played it over and over, and felt like their singer Kevin Rowland was singing just to me, and their Number One, Geno, about an old American soul singer called Geno Washington was ace. Rick loved it, I mean really loved it, and when the 'groovy vicar' played it at Crutchfield, boy, could Rick dance, even copied the way Dexy's dressed, donkey jacket, skull cap, black trousers with DM Shoes, he really got it, that's what he's like, changing his look but always looking Mod. He wore a baseball jacket the other day, nicked it from his brother, with a blue Ben Sherman shirt and jeans, looked good, the Ivy League look he calls it, got the idea from our bible, Richard Barnes' Mods! He calls himself an Ivy League Mod, first one round here, that's Rick for you, original and that's why I like him.

I like Tom as well, but we do argue a lot, my mother says that is because we are alike, still trying to work out what she means by that. I like going round his house as well to listen to his music and look at his clothes and I used to get a second dinner there as his mother would invite me to stay and eat. But Tom called my mother, not me my mother, and said I was going round at dinner time and I must come before or after, she fucking agreed with him and told me off. I couldn't believe that he'd 'grassed' on me. Back to Tom, he is well dressed, and very knowledgeable on music, I am jealous, no, well yes in a way, but it gives me someone to compete with, so I guess my mother is right.

It was Tom that played me The Beatles' song Taxman from their LP Revolver, reckoning that Weller nicked the idea for Start. I said "influenced him", we nearly came to blows, only for his father to break it up and I was chucked out, came home screaming and shouting. My father made me call him to say sorry, telling me sometimes "you have to take the higher ground." He, Tom that is, not my father, did introduce me to a sixties band The Action, produced by George Martin, who produced The Beatles. Some call him the fifth Beatle, whilst others call their manager Brian Epstein the fifth Beatle, I don't think there was a fifth Beatle, they were The Fab Four, say no more. The album he's got is called Ultimate Action, Paul Weller wrote the sleeve notes, really good soulful sound, a bit like The Small Faces meets the Who, with a bit of Motown. Tom did me a tape and all the time reminds me how he got me into The Action, even told my brother, why? I have no idea.

But I was the first to get The Creation LP. I saw their single on the All Mod Cons sleeve notes and the teenagers in Tower Records ordered We Are Paintermen, cost me a bit of money and I had to borrow it from my parents. Tom went spare, he even started kicking the wall when I turned up one Saturday morning with it, plus I had this blue raincoat on which my mother got from a jumble sale and with a bit of her magic on the sewing machine I looked like Steve Marriott. We played the LP, as his mother did a round of sausage sandwiches for us, which annoyed Tom even more. Vinnie told me during the summer; if you see your 'enemy' get annoyed keep going as they will get madder, good advice.

We listened to We Are Paintermen and recognised the song Painter Man. A disco band, Boney M from Germany, two black girls and one black bloke did this, saw them on Top of The Pops, liked the song. My brother said, after watching the show, it was about Adolf Hitler as he wanted to be a painter and ended up becoming the leader of Nazi Germany and nearly taking over the World. I believed him for a long time, even told my mates at Nursery Road, and they believed me, then I heard the original, just shows you can't believe everything someone tells you. I like The Creation's sound, very much like The Who but a little more pop and soulful, and I like the fact that I got there before Tom.

We've started going to Carnaby Street on the last Friday of our school holidays, even half terms. It's our going back to school day, cushions the blow before we do bleeding go back. Tom and Rick seem to be doing all right at school or so they tell me. I just don't get teachers, I learn more from the books, magazines and music papers I read, the films and TV programmes I watch, the music I listen to. Anyway school for me is something between the holidays and mucking about. Going clothes shopping gives us something to look forward to, we start saving up, get Birthday or Christmas money advances and think about what we are going to buy. We meet other Mods, chat, share cigarettes, nice feeling, but we have to avoid the Skinheads, just like Pemberton, but worse looking, green flight jackets, bleached jeans and high ox blood DM's, some with tattoos on their faces like a tear or a spider's web, seen one with a big dark rat on his shoulder. They like picking on kids like us. Lucky we haven't been hit yet, been asked for a fag or ten pence outside Oxford Street Tube, I've been spat on, once, but we leave Carnaby Street usually around 3 O'clock, as I think they come out of the pubs then, usually drunk or go looking for more glue. They sniff glue, pour into bags, sit in an alleyway and sniff it, fuck that, the smell makes me sick, and apparently it's the smell that gets you high.

Rick got his nose broken in Kingston by Skinheads outside Jack Brendon's the other week. He had popped down one Saturday morning to look for some Monkey Boots, like DM boots but smarter. Looking through the window he felt a light tap on his shoulder, turned round and smack - bastards. They seem to hate blacks, pakis, the lot, they're part of this political party called The National Front, who hate all foreigners. When I first met Rick he said he was National Front until one of the black twins from Rydens roughed him up a bit at Crutchfield. Now he's the other way, as you know he loves his reggae music. My brother said he has been to a few gigs where the Skinheads have turned up and Sieg Heiled like a Nazi solider in the Second World War. They just like trouble, all the time, whilst it seems Mods only fight when they have to, Skinheads fight all the time and for fun, hate them and I am scared of them.

We always go to a shop in the main area called The Flea Market; it's like an indoor market with loads of shops with the best shop at the top of the first floor Robot. It's packed with loads of clothes, like a jumble sale only better. Tom bought a Blue Parka there, the Asian shop keeper said it was a genuine RAF one whilst Vinnie and I said to him it was dyed; he wouldn't believe us and tells everyone that it's a rare RAF parka. One thing that Tom and I love are the Mod fanzines; Extraordinary Sensations, Direction, Reaction and Maximum Speed. Magazines written by Mods for Mods, Paul Weller, Ian Page, Chris Pope, Billy Hassett, Buddy from The Chords, and Bob and the rest of The Purple Hearts all give interviews, what a great way to meet our heroes. Robot has them all.

Tom, me and Mott have talked about doing a fanzine, but we argue over the title. Tom wants to call it The Dreams of Children. Mott, We Are The Mods, and me, A Shattered Mirror, a true reflection of Mod. Mine is the best and the most original, and Tom wants to be the editor, as do I, as does Mott, and we won't agree on being co-editors. Rick said he would contribute whilst Vinnie says he will use it as toilet paper, but we need to sort out the title and who runs it, before we can do that. A new magazine came out during the summer The Face, first issue had an interview with Jerry Dammers from The Specials and issue 2 had a great interview with Paul Weller, who was wearing a red denim jacket with a sheriff badge. Tom and I saw a similar jacket in Robot, and both went to grab it at the same time, we had a fight in the shop, which was egged on by Vinnie and Rick. Mott tried to act the peace maker, he thinks he's our father when he comes out with us, but I reckon he wanted to buy it. But I am happy to say the shop keeper sold it me as he could see my passion was stronger than Tom's, who stormed out of the shop shouting something about it being rightfully his and it would be wasted on me, the other Mods in the shop all laughed including us lot, apart from Mott. You see if your friend gets something before you, that's it, you can't copy him, you just don't look good or original, but it's OK to copy Weller, Marriott, Townsend or Page.

We eventually found Tom in a small burger bar nearby, oddly enough eating a burger and looking very annoyed, he refused to show what he had bought, well, until Vinnie and I stole the bag and ran off. As we ran off we could hear him screaming our names and again he was met by laughter. As I said, badges are now a big no no, but Weller wearing this sheriff badge gave me the idea to get my Man from Uncle badge out and wear it on my new red denim jacket, which I love wearing in front of Tom.

The other shop we all love is Shelley's, get all our shoes from there, got a great burgundy pair of Jam shoes and light blue bowling shoes, I did want all-white bowling shoes, but Tom got them before me. He sneaked off to Carnaby Street one Saturday on his own to get them, bastard. My mother won't let me go to London on my own and if I did she would find out, she always does. So when Tom wore them we got into another fight 'cos Vinnie spurred me on to step on them and scuff them up, Vinnie was jumping up and down laughing. Our fights usually last for about 30 seconds, more scuffles than punching, no one ever wins

The Face was really good at first, all Mod, Two Tone and Punk but now it's about this new trend, called Blitz Kids, what the fuck does that mean, something from the war when German planes bombed cities in England, my English grandparents talk about that a lot. These Blitz Kids all dress like they are going to some fancy dress party, men in wedding type dresses with fucking clown make up. I don't get it and trust me, you know that I get youth culture, but this makes no fucking sense, and the music is total and utter shit. I know I am swearing lot, but I'm so annoyed. No guitars, organs or trumpets but synths, electronic stuff, no depth, no soul. It won't last, it's like when skateboards were what every kid wanted, then after six months they were back on their push bikes again. From reading about it, it's geezers and girls in their late teens and early 20s, going to clubs in London, dressed like ponces and that's it, one of the bands is OK, Spandau Ballet, they look good and could be good Mods, shame.

On a brighter note, I have seen The Jam twice, first time at Hammersmith Odeon and the second time at Guildford Civic; well what can I say... a lot. The first one was, as I said, Hammersmith Odeon, November last year and they were promoting their fifth LP, Sound Effects, which was to come out later that month.

My brother bought himself, me and a spare ticket for a friend as an advanced Christmas present, as long as he went with me. My parents wouldn't let me go on my own. I wanted to see The Jam before Tom, so I didn't ask him instead I asked Susie from school. I was quite nervous, in fact shaking when I did, took about 10 minutes before I got to the point, and she said yes, with her radiant smile. If I could have somersaulted I would have done, instead I just smiled for ages until her friend Tina said I looked like a clown from Billy Smart's circus. Susie isn't a Mod, but she does dress well, dresses like a smart punk, she's a fan of Siouxsie and the Banshees, Blondie and a band that's really big at the moment Adam and The Ants, the lead singer Adam Ant thinks he's a Red Indian and their music sounds like American tribal music, you know the sort you hear in Westerns. I pretend I like them as I don't want to upset her and give her a reason to dislike me. But she loves The Jam, told me that when she saw me down Crutchfield I reminded her of Paul Weller, I was going for the Ian Page look but I wasn't going to argue.

The journey seemed to take forever, been to London on the train and by car, but this was Hammersmith, so had to change here and there. Had to walk through this underpass and as we got to the top there were loads of Skinheads, mean, brutal and nasty looking ones outside this arcade, they all shouted at us. I ignored them, as did my brother and Susie. Anyway when we got in the Odeon there were loads of Mods, I mean loads, all well dressed, even saw TV presenter Gary Crowley, he does a TV show White Light and The Fun Factory, with all the bands, he's got a real cockney accent, talks a million miles an hour, my brother said hello and he said hello back, and he even smiled at me, again when I told Tom, we had another fight. My brother reckons deep down we enjoy it. I was hoping to have a beer but my brother promised my parents he would only buy us coca cola, bastard.

The seats we had were a bit at the back, but a good view of the stage. A band called The Dolly Mixtures opened up, from a distance they looked quite pretty, but I couldn't really hear what they were singing, as most of Mods were shouting at them. Then after that it was about 30 minutes or so, the lights dimmed, I was so excited, exchanged glances and smiles with my brother, Susie and a few other Mods. It felt like I had been waiting for this moment all my life, to see Paul, Bruce and Rick play, then a grey haired man with the look of an old Teddy Boy, Paul's father and their manager John Weller, walked on stage and shouted out "Put your hands together for the best fucking band in the world…The Jam." Just one sentence, I suppose that's all it needed, and then bang a musical explosion, power and attitude, they opened with a new song Dream Time.

I was in heaven, taken into another world, my eyes don't leave the stage, The Jam, as they always do, giving it their all, playing with passion, and us, the fans love it, really love, we are an army, a true fucking army, a Mod revolution. They do a few hits, songs from Setting Sons and the new album, love Pretty Green and do a long version of Eton Rifles, feeding back guitar, Weller screaming something into the microphone, puts the guitar on his knee and starts spinning round, loved the yellow shirt he was wearing. I want to be in a band, I want to create music like this, The Jam don't just entertain us, they inspire us, educate us, unite us. The lights came on, I hugged Susie, she hugged me back. I got a tingle inside. I chatted to some other Mods as I was walking out they didn't seem to care that I was younger than them; they could see my love for The Jam. I told them it's the first time, they liked that, a few said me and Susie looked good together, which made me happy.

Getting home was far from fun. Outside the tube station (at midnight) were loads of horrible Skinheads, we walked past them. I grabbed Susie's hand as all of a sudden I felt the need to protect her. My brother felt the same as he stepped in front of us so they would hit him first. One of the evil Skinheads looked at us and said "Leave them, get the ones with boating blazers." I felt sorry for any Mods with boating blazers, but there were some tough looking Mods in there tonight. My brother isn't really a Mod anymore, dresses like a band called Joy Division, chat about that later. Anyway we get inside the tube station, my brother tells us to get whatever tube comes next, then we hear a massive bang and a fight starts to break out, my brother and me, still holding Susie's hand, run past the ticket collector who pulls away and lets us through. I look over my shoulder and see the Skinheads go in and I am pleased to say the Mods fight back, see one Skinhead hit the floor, its madness, Vinnie would have loved this.

Luckily the first tube that comes in is for Earl's Court, as we needed to get there to change for Wimbledon. None of us talked, but I was thinking why can't those fucking Skinheads do something better with their lives. We get to Earl's Court thinking it's over, wrong, England were playing at Wembley that night, and there were loads of England supporters all over Earls Courts, singing, well more like shouting whilst drinking loads of booze. They aren't Mods, Skinheads or Soul Boys, just long haired yobos; they shouted a few things at us. All we had done was go out to see our favourite band, not harming anyone. The Skinheads and these yobs made me realise why Weller wrote Down In The Tube Station At Midnight - it's scary. A few came over to us, one who seemed to be the leader asked where had we been, my brother told him, he said he loved The Jam, and started singing Going Underground.

All in A Good Day's

He was holding a bottle of cider, which he passed to my brother, but not me. I felt I really needed a drink, now I understood when my father has had a 'hard day' pours himself a scotch. The other England supporters saw we were getting on and left us alone. Once we got to Wimbledon everything was safe, my brother made sure Susie and I were OK and went to the phone box to call my father to pick us up from Walton Station. Anyway the next day at school I made out I stood with the Mods, everyone believed me. I hate lying to them but I suppose you have to lie from time to time, to get on.

The next time I saw The Jam was December and Sound Affects was out. An amazing record, dark, sinister yet beautiful, played it over and over again, and the back sleeve notes had a poem by Shelley, Mask of Anarchy, so I popped down to WH Smiths in Walton to get a book of his poetry. You ain't going to believe this, Tom was there, doing the same, so we had another fight, we both got chucked out and banned, then I went to the library and yes he was there as well, I think you know the rest. In the end, my brother got a copy of Shelley's complete works. Even before I read it I phoned Tom to tell him, who shouted and put the phone down on me.

There's a lovely love song called Monday on Sound Affects, Weller can write some nice love songs, Fly, I Need You, surprises me, 'cos he looks so mean. When I heard it for the first time, I thought of Susie and still do. This time, I went with my friends, Tom, Rick and Mott, Vinnie refused to go, stating he would rather die than see The Jam play. They were playing at the Guildford Civic, which is just past Woking and near us, 20 to 30 minutes by train or about 20 minutes by car, 'depending on traffic' as my father would say. As you know, we are still very young and none of our parents wanted us going without a 'responsible adult', even though Mott believed he was. Jesus, he is old before his time, I'm sure by the time he's 16 he will be wearing slippers and sitting by a log fire, "Put on the kettle and make some tea, It's all a part of feeling groovie, Put on your slippers turn on the TV, It's all a part of feeling groovie" Smithers Jones spot on.

81

Rick's mum took us and Tom's dad picked us up. Rick's mother totally embarrassed us as she wouldn't drop us off round the corner, she wanted to make sure we got into the venue safely. What does she do, she pulls up right in front of these older Mods, boys and girls, we are left with no choice but to get out and we are greeted by loud laughs and cutting remarks, "make sure you wash behind your ears" "tell the teacher if any of the older boys pick on you" "don't forget your dinner money", we walk to the entrance with red faces and our heads down. We were all togged up hoping to impress the Mod boys and flirt with the Mod girls, but instead we looked like the supporting cast from Just William, thanks to Rick's mother, Margaret.

Vinnie found this amusing and wouldn't shut up about it for ages. It was a big mistake to have told him. Once inside we mingled, but a few Mods throughout the night were pointing at us and sniggering. Before The Jam came on Tom went to the phone box, called his Dad, whose name is John, he's a bank manager, he's OK to us, not over friendly. I couldn't hear Tom but I watched him and I could see he was going bonkers, as if he was telling 'John' to pick us up round the corner.

Anyway the gig was out of this world, and when The Jam did Pretty Green, Weller introduced it by saying "this song is about Michael Jackson and the Bank of England", I have no idea what he meant by that, but it sounded good, and then seemed to do encore after encore ending with their version of the soul classic, Heatwave, with Weller just in shorts and black tape across his nipples. Yes, he and the rest of The Jam have influenced me in terms of dress sense, music and ideas, but there is no fucking way I am going to go for that look, never….., who's the face now lads. Believe it or not, Tom and I hugged at the end of the night, as we were so happy, but I did whisper in his ear this was my second Jam gig, and only his first, but I think The Jam had blown him away to get him annoyed, that's the magic of Paul, Bruce and Rick.

But Tom and the boys did go and see Secret Affair there in September, I couldn't go. Even though school had started we went on a late family holiday to Italy to celebrate my uncle's birthday, no not Bill, that's on my mother's side, this was Zio Franco, in English Uncle Frank. We went to his holiday villa, a place called Stresa on this huge lake called Maggiore, near Milan. It's beautiful, hills and woodlands, wonderful views, read Shelley lived in Italy, I would live there and have a flat in London when I become a pop star or a writer. It's nice to get away and to be honest to forget about being a Mod. I know if they heard me say this I would be hanged, drawn and quartered. I was a little upset to miss Secret Affair and my mother could see I was, so she got my uncle to drive us to Milan and we went shopping. She treated me to a lovely red jumper with a white stripe across it and a short sleeved black button down, all the way from Italy, in fact they are my best clothes.

By all accounts the Secret Affair gig was something else, they wouldn't stop talking or boasting about it, especially Tom. Secret Affair brought a single out last summer My World, got in the Top Twenty, should have been Number One, written by Dave Cairns not Page and Cairns. It has an orchestra at the start, that makes the hairs on the back of your neck stand up, Page's voice comes in, so beautiful and soulful, "I can feel that taste for life slipping away, And striking the lost chord I find nothing new to say, Someone told me all dressed with nowhere to go, I should have that sinking feeling, my head hung low" it's reassurance that Mod is still strong and Secret Affair are still here.   The Jam played some secret gigs earlier this year in Woking, a lot of the older Mods went, like Snowy and even my brother. One was on a Saturday and the other two Monday and Tuesday, whilst we were at fucking school, none of our parents would let us take the day off. We heard that at one of these gigs Weller was so drunk he couldn't play, not sure if I would like to have seen that. Oh yeah, forgot to say Charlie Cairoli died last year, just before The Jam got to Number One with Going Underground. Was watching the news with my family when they announced it, we all looked at my father, he showed no emotion, he just poured himself a whisky and went upstairs. After reading up on The Beatles, my father was the Pete Best of the

Clown world. Best was sacked by The Beatles before they made it big, just as my father was sacked by Charlie Cairoli before he made it big. As he was in his bedroom, I went into my room, and put on The Beat's "Tears of a Clown", a few bars in, my father shouted out "turn it fucking off"

VIII

A Bag of Chips

The Purple Hearts have a song *Millions Like Us*, a powerful aggressive song, with a sort of punk feel, telling the World, well England, there are Mods everywhere. Love it, as does Tom, whilst not so much Rick, he is getting into America blues music, he's played me a few songs, I like the grit and the bleakness of it, music for lost souls, while soul music seems to be a celebration. Rick also played me a new band he's discovered, Nine Below Zero, a new blues band from London, great sound, fast blues loud and hard, they dress in nice three button suits, look very Mod. Rick and his brother are off to see them soon at the Hammersmith Odeon, I am in no hurry to go there again, still he didn't invite me, in fact he's going with Mott, bastard. But he's written down a few blues artists for me to buy, Howlin' Wolf, Muddy Waters, tells me they influenced the early Rolling Stones. My brother told me about The Yardbirds, a British band from the Sixties, a sort of blues with a Who edge. Found an album in WH Smith, cheap as chips, have this song *Train Kept A'Rollin*, love it, played it to Rick, he nodded, just nodded, and said "Fine", no madness like leaping in the air, Tom would, yet I do admire the way Rick holds back, you never know what he's really thinking. Never play any music to Vinnie, nor does he play any to me, apart from The Beatles, but he said he likes Nine Below Zero, I was shocked, as he seems to be so disinterested in music.

Going back to *Millions Like Us*, that's how I feel on a Saturday in Walton. It started off with a handful of us, Christopher, before he stopped being a Mod, Mott, but he doesn't bother anymore, and me, Vinnie, Rick and Tom hanging out in the centre, not doing much, just us being us. Word soon spread, can you believe it, a small suburban town has become a place for Mods, not just our age, but even older Mods, mainly from Addlestone, they come down on their scooters, they call themselves The Virgin Soldiers. Really nice Lambrettas and Vespas with all the chrome and mirrors, nice paint jobs on the side panels. I like them, but Vinnie really loves them, keeps talking about getting his scooter, he wants both makes, I think that's what he likes most about the Mod scene, the scooters.

They are all faces these Virgin Soldiers, heard they like a fight, they talk to us, think they like these young Mods looking up to them. It was great one Saturday, when about 10 to 15 of them came down on their scooters on the way to London, saw them pulling into the centre and as they were getting off their scooters I started singing out loud *Millions Like Us*, then everyone, well everyone who was a Mod and was there, joined in. I got a massive sense of pride, made me happy, so happy I am Mod. And it's not just Mods who come down, girls from Rydens and Heathside, and real rich posh girls who live in St George's Hill and go to Notre Dame School come down a lot, most of them fancy Vinnie and a few others, not sure about me, I think they find me a little too intense, as I talk about a Mod revolution but I don't care, as I've got Susie, she's my 'sunshine girl'.

Just think a couple of years ago I was a scruffy kid in cheap clothes, wanting and hoping so much to be a Mod, now I, well me and my mates, have become a 'tourist attraction'. Got a good life outside of school, Crutchfield Friday, Walton Town Saturday and Sunday, perhaps an afternoon round Rick's or Tom's or mine listening to music and chatting all things Mod, then bed and ready for bleeding school, but by Monday morning break I am having a laugh with the boys.

86

A Bag of Chips

I went into Walton early the other day to pick something up from Boots for my mother, popped into WH Smiths, the ban after my fight with Tom had lifted, to get the NME and Nathan Swine was there, remember him? He was reading a copy of Mayfair from the top shelf; no shop assistant had the bottle to tell him to put it back. He's a Skinhead, no surprise there, I hadn't seen him since the horse incident with Mickey Davies, and had forgotten all about him, after my father stopped getting the 'cheap' whisky from his dad. I froze for a second, then he smiled and spoke to me, he invited me next door to the Baker's Oven to have a coffee and a jam doughnut, I ate one, he ate three, he paid, with a roll of five pound notes just like his dad.

Nathan told me he was a Mod for a while then became a Skinhead because he preferred the music; I think he meant the aggro. He went on to say he didn't miss leaving Nursery Road but the Council tracked him down so he had to go back to school, only to be expelled for beating up a teacher. I liked that, now he's at some special school until he's 16, maybe I could go there. He even flashed his ash, (gave me a cigarette), going to Crutchfield makes you smoke. I have to admit I really liked talking to him, wished he had been like that at school, we could have been friends. As we left and said goodbye, Vinnie was coming up the High Street with some new additions to Mods, Mark Harris and David Jennings from a nearby posh school Halliford. I think one lives in Thames Ditton the other in Shepperton, but I don't really care, I don't mind them, but not bothered about being their mates.

"Talking to a Skinhead?"

"Old friend Vinnie, a long time ago."

"You can't be friends with a Skinhead" he snaps back

Mark and David look at me like I was a traitor, who are they? Sporting a Parka and bog standard Sta Press, with a few Jam albums to match. I could tell by Vinnie's tone and face he was just joking. I have just learnt to smile back and that way he stops annoying if he thinks you are not upset, otherwise he will go on and on until you crack, and he's worse where there is a crowd to play to, and believe me I have gone barmy sometimes. So we all walk off to annoy some innocent shopper or do some small shoplifting, sweets from Woolworths or records or magazines from WH Smiths, handy to have a Parka. Vinnie and I have got quite good, but the master is a kid called Mint, quite daring, stole some aftershave, silk ties and handkerchiefs the other day from Grant Warden's, Walton's answer to Harrods, a posh departmental store right next to the centre, which has this abstract art statue outside, which no one young or old, can work out what it is.

They have a bit of an upmarket café, The Bay Tree. When we've got enough money we go there for a cup of tea or even a cake, been chucked out a few times, and had a few bans, think I've now been banned from every shop in Walton apart from Tower Records, as that is our church. Usually the girls from Notre Dame call in at The Bay Tree as they have the money, I don't mind it there but I prefer the Bakers Oven or The Wimpy at the end of the High Street, just has more of a teen feel to it.

We have a Safeway's in the town centre. When we moved to Walton my brother got a Saturday job there, served Jimmy Pursey from Sham 69, got his autograph and stuck it on The *Adventures of the Hersham Boys* album, he was over the moon. So was I. Anyway their fruit and vegetable stand is right by the window and the other day some chap was shopping with his mother, or could have been his wife, picking apples, Vinnie tapped on the window, and said "not that one, pick that one", the man laughed and carried on picking, I joined in, again he laughed and carried on, we followed him down as he moved onto the potatoes, and we did the same, now we could see he was getting annoyed, bad for him but good for us. As he moved down to the carrots, we did the same, this time no laughter, he threw down the carrots, kicked the shopping trolley, knocked the woman he was with over and ran towards the door, my God, he wanted our blood. We stood for a minute, made sure we had eye contact; we were up for the chase. There he stood, panting and grunting, scruffy man, no sense of style and certainly no sense of humour, our eyes met and then Vinnie shouted out

"Everything You Want from a Store and a Little Bit More", these words sent him totally and utterly insane, we started to laugh, bad idea when you are about to run as the laughter can slow you down.

Yet this was just so funny and he didn't look like he could run a marathon, eat one maybe, perhaps even two of them. He pulls off his mac, our cue to run, but I was wrong about his health, this man could sprint, so we doubled our speed, looking over our shoulder in doing so we failed to notice PC 'Ginger' MacDonald, as you know the biggest bastard copper, coming round the corner. When we noticed the bastard Vinnie tries to go left and I try to go right, but 'ole ginger has got arms like Mr. Fantastic from The Fantastic Four, he stretched out, grabbed us and pulled us in tight, locked his arms round our skinny little necks, we struggled but the more we struggled the tighter he pulled his grip, the mad shopper quickly went from being bonkers to an innocent bystander.

"These boys have been harassing me officer."

"I am sorry to hear that sir, would you like to lodge a complaint so we can arrest these culprits, we've had our eye on them for some time and it's only been a question of time."

Vinnie and I exchanged glances, charged with what, helping him with which fruit and vegetables to choose, the man nodded his head but before he could get a word out the woman whom he knocked over arrived looking rather flustered and said "Malcolm, these boys were mucking about, you are too sensitive for your own good."

Malcolm's face went red, but Ginger wanted our blood "Madam, please…."

This woman is our saviour, "No," she cuts him off short, "My son", we start to giggle, Ginger throttles our necks a little more, "won't be pressing charges, so I request you release these boys immediately." I liked her, slowly Ginger lets us go, we both smile at the woman, as we do at Malcolm, but the smile to him is cheeky, then we turned and faced our policeman friend with two massive beaming smiles, he just snarled and walked forward, as he did that he purposely stepped on our toes, "ow" we both yelped.

"There was no need for that" said the woman in our support

"Sorry Madam, accidents do happen" he replied in a sarcastic tone. Of course they do, been reading about kids having enough of the police, especially places like Brixton. Only last month they fought the police when they let a black kid called Michael Bailey bleed to death. I could see Ginger letting us bleed to death, seems the Old Bill really hate the black kids in London, have this law called the 'Sus Law', watched a debate programme the other day, where these kids, mainly black, were having a go at the police in a TV studio. 'Sus Law' means the Old Bill can stop and search ya when they feel like it, they must love it. The woman shook her head then opened her purse, Malcolm was about to say something, but he was cut short "Shut up Malcolm", and she passed us a pound note, we smiled, said gee thanks, nodded at Ginger and headed towards the Wimpy for some chips and coke. That's pretty much our Saturday.

So as you have gathered, we have our admirers and of course our enemies - Skinheads, Soul Boys, Punks and the local police, tribes of roughly the same age, and the Authority, but we now have a new enemy, the Pub Man. What's a Pub Man? Idiots, men who seem to be over the age of 25, "And those golden faces are under 25", they could be younger, but they look older. They dress smart, well in their eyes, plain dark trousers, black, dark blue or grey, black or brown shoes, light coloured shirts or V-neck jumpers, sometimes with no top underneath. In the summer, they wear light jackets or fake leather ones and in the winter they wear sheepskin coats. They seriously think they look the business, but to us they look like Dennis Waterman from Minder, sure that's their idol. They march to the pub, I mean really march like it's a mission clutching their 20 Benson and Hedges with their gold plated lighter, it's got to be gold plated, as they don't look the sort to carry a solid gold lighter.

They think they are Rudolph Valentino, but we've never seen them with a girl, well occasionally, overweight birds, really two ton Tessie's. What makes it funny we sometimes see them holding hands, like they've pulled Lynda Carter from Wonder Woman. I think they hate us 'cos they are jealous of us.

There's about four of them, two with black hair, one with brown and one with blonde, now he really does look like Dennis Waterman, and from a distance we always sing "I could be so good for you" from Minder, and in return he does the wanker sign. Then the warfare started with the pub men. Vinnie, me, Rick and Mint, forgot to say Mint looks like Sting from The Police, with his bleached blonde hair he's always met by us singing The Police's Roxanne, which he just laughs about. I do like his take on Mod, often wears a grandad shirt, no collar, and sleeveless jumper, with boating shoes and light Jeans, looks good. I wouldn't go for it, but I did buy a grandad shirt the other day in Kingston, just haven't worn it out yet. We are chatting outside WH Smiths, in fact talking about football, but since I've become a Mod football isn't a big thing with me, but still watch Match of The Day and the FA Cup Final. Mint is good at football, supports Fulham and reckons he will get a trial with them soon, hopefully before he stands trial for shoplifting, he can't help himself.

One of the dark haired ones looks like Luke Duke from The Dukes of Hazzard, even wears the odd checkered shirt. We, as in the Mods, not the pub men, go home early on Saturday to watch Dukes of Hazzard when it's on, the programme is shit, but their cousin Daisy Duke is something else, I shudder and get excited thinking about her. Tom loves her, he has a scrap book with loads of photos of Daisy Duke he has collected and cut out, hard to look through as a lot of the pages stick together. Anyway, Luke Duke hears us talking, bumps into Mint, "Fulham are shit, and their supporters are shit"

"Fuck off" Mint replies, Luke hits him and hits him hard. Mint hits the floor, Vinnie goes to kick him, Luke sees this, grabs his leg and pushes him to the ground, Luke takes a swing at me, he misses but I stumble back bump into Rick and we both fall down, all four of us, on the floor, "bloody Mods" he yells and walks off.

Later in the week Rick and I told Snowy about it when we

saw him coming out of Tower Records. Snowy told us that Luke Duke's name is Jimmy Thomas, knows karate, said better we keep away, and when he can will have a word, somehow I don't think Snowy will, he seemed scared of him. We see them drinking in these horrible pubs, The George or The Duke's Head, all near the centre, they sit by the window, sipping their pints, we like to chuck small stones at the window whilst they drink, they look at us and move away, there is tension in the air, you know what, I love it. Today, I am treating Vinnie to Fish 'n' Chips at the sit down one in Bridge Street, he treated me to a Wimpy the other week, so it's my turn, got my mother's luncheon vouchers. Mint is with us, as is Paul Fuld, simply called Fuld, he's been a Mod for a while and goes to the same school as Vinnie, I've only started to get to know him and wish I knew him last year. Listen to this, his mother works at the Volvo dealership just by Walton Bridge, and believe it or not, Bruce as in Bruce Foxton, came down to buy his car, just after *Start* had got to Number One. It made the local rag, The Informer, couldn't believe it when I saw that, a member of The Jam buying a car in Walton-on- Thames, my new home town. Fuld knew about it, but as the other Mods at Heathside, Tom and Rick, were always taking the piss he didn't invite them to the showroom just this lanky one, called Martin. They got to meet and have a chat with Bruce, even had their photo taken with him and got his autograph, fucking hell. After that, they accepted him, and now he gives as good as he gets. Tom was in tears when he heard about Bruce popping down, Vinnie found it funny and couldn't care less. I like Fuld, friendly and funny, not bad in his dress sense, a bit basic, Hush Puppies, Jeans and Fred Perry's, but he looks good and is popular with the girls as he has the face of an angel.

I don't mind Mint and Fuld tagging along, always up for a laugh, but I am not treating them, as my father always tells me "never be the first to get a round in with strangers." Not sure if that means don't be taken for a ride or he just doesn't like buying someone a drink. They aren't bothered, Mint and Fuld always have money, I think Mint steals from his mother's purse, whilst Fuld helps his father out, who's a plumber, when he can. It's just nice to sit down with my best mate and two good mates over a plate of cod and chips, yet the day doesn't go according to plan, in fact far from it.

As we are just about to enter the shop, we hear "So you think I look like Dennis Waterman," we turn round all at the same time, there he is, looking like Terry from Minder, open neck shirt with his cheap gold plated (you know they don't own real gold) medallion showing, tight jeans slightly flared at the end, brown pointed shoes with a bit of a high heel, light blonde hair that is a cross between a mob top and a side parting whilst clutching his beloved 20 Bensons and 'industry standard' lighter. With a vision like this and his opening statement, we start to laugh.

Old Dennis wasn't expecting this, he wanted us to run or apologise, so runs straight over to Mint, hits him but he doesn't go down. The Pub Men always seem to go for Mint first; he must just have one of those faces. Vinnie outraged, throws a punch, he's been doing boxing for a bit now and his dad used to box, what a punch, it hits him straight on the jaw, Dennis hits the floor one punch...Pow.

Mint sees the chap on the floor and quickly sticks in the boot, fast and hard just like a footballer, Dennis yelps, I see my chance and follow Mint as does Fuld, as I start to kick him I start singing *"If you want to, I'll change the situation, Right people, right time, just the wrong location, I've got a good idea, just you keep me near, I'd be so good for you,"* it's the lyrics from the Minder theme tune, in case you didn't know. The others all smile and join in, we've been watching this show for ages, don't think there's one kid who doesn't know the words, and when we get to the main chorus, "I could be so good for you" we kick even harder with every 'I could be so good for you.' Impossible for Dennis to get up as he's being bombarded by the boots of the young Mods, shoppers stop and stare, seeing these kids giving a Dennis Waterman look alike a good kicking whilst singing the Minder theme tune, real live pop art.... Then we hear "Charlie... Charlie ", we look up and see local tough nut Jimmy Thomas, oh fuck, he looks annoyed.

Thomas starts running towards us and fast, we stop kicking Dennis, who isn't moving. Then Thomas leaps in the air, pushes his right leg out and his leg behind his back, thinking he's Grasshopper from Kung Fu. We ain't no real experts in fighting but we can see in advance what he is going to do, so we all move out of the way, then like Cato from The Pink Panther films, he whizzes right past and his battle cry of "Hyah!" goes to a scream of "Fuck!" as he smashes into the plate glass window of the fish 'n' chip shop, it's over in seconds.

There are massive loud screams from women and children and yelps from the men as Thomas crashes through, landing on a table, glass flies out everywhere, we all cover our faces. For about a second or two it seemed like the whole world had stopped, as we all exchange glances between the customers and us. We look over and Dennis is slowly picking himself up, but he doesn't look like he's up for a fight, then Thomas moves, oh good, he's not dead, but hurt. We hear him groan as he places both feet from the table onto the floor, he sits up straight brushing off the broken glass. He stands up straight but then starts to wobble, he has a few cuts round the face, nothing bad, he looks at us, but nothing, no threats or even fear, just looks at us in disbelief, then he collapses, as he does so we hear the police sirens. "Leggit" shouts Vinnie; I really don't think he needs to ask.   We all start to run up Bridge Street towards the town centre, as we are running about eight to ten of the Merry Mod gang led by Rick and Tom are heading towards us. Someone must have said we were heading towards the fish and chip shop, but I don't really have the time to think about that now.

"Old Bill" yells Mint as we run towards them. Now this has got nothing to do them, they could have quite easily carried on going about their business, but no, they decide to join us and start running with us in the direction of the town centre, Mods stick together, as Snowy once told us. I hear, well we all hear, the slamming of car doors, I look over my shoulder as do many of the others and see four coppers get out of two panda cars, blocking all one way traffic in Bridge Street, thinking it's better to catch us on foot but we know all the nooks and crannies of the town.

As we get to the end of the street by Woolworths, we see an army of coppers all on foot, well running through the town centre to our right. I never knew Walton had so many Old Bill, they must sleep all day and wait for the call, just like Thunderbirds. But there's no sign of Ginger Macdonald, he must be on holiday, or having a wank. "Left" I scream, everyone follows my command, I like that, but Vinnie pushes to the front to lead the troops, as he does he gives me a look as if to say I give the orders.

am a cocktail of emotions, fear, the police in pursuit, anger; all I wanted to do was have some fish 'n' chips with my mates. But we stood up for ourselves against the Pub Men, but the police won't see it like that. Then I'm embarrassed as I see my beautiful Susie with Tina, Michelle and Liz from school on the opposite side of the road. Well Liz goes to Heathside but at this moment in time that isn't really important. They must have heard where we were having lunch, the girls all stop in their tracks and look at these running Mods, I sheepishly give Susie a wave, and she returns the gesture slowly with no smile, but a look of confusion. Fuck it, the girl of my dreams seeing me being chased like a junkie by Kojak and Crocker through the back streets of New York.

We steam across the road, with the cars slamming on their brakes, and a few bumpers smacking each other. Shouts of "yobbos" "bring back National Service" "hang the little bastards" "fucking Mods" fly through the air from outraged motorists and disgruntled shoppers. Vinnie leads us to St Mary's Church, which has an alley that runs through the graveyard and takes you onto Churchfield Road and from there, there are about three or four different ways we can go, it's good for me, as I live ten minutes away, if I get home before I get nicked I could make out I've been home all day reading.

The police are making ground, as we speed up and enter the

churchyard, there standing before us is a bride and groom with all the in-laws, brothers, sisters, aunts, uncles, grandparents and snotty nosed kids all dressed up but still looking like shit, standing proud for the family album wedding photo. They are smiling at first, then they see the army of Mods stampeding towards them, we can't stop, we won't stop, I move to my right on the graves, as do Vinnie and Fuld, but the others, maybe they are suspicious about stepping on graves, stay on the path. The men of the wedding break away from the photo, and try and stop "Vinnie's army", the Mods fight back, pushing over or hitting or both to anyone that stands in the way. I see Mint chin the photographer, one punch and he's down, then Mint tries to take his camera out of his hand, as he is doing that I see loads of blue jacket arms pull him to the ground, he's nicked. The Old Bill have arrived in numbers, swinging their beloved and trusted truncheons, not just at the Mods but also at the Wedding party, There are screams, shouts everywhere. I slowly stop to watch, then I feel a strong tug "Come on," it's Fuld, good old solid Paul. The ruckus has bought us time, as the Old Bill are busy fighting everyone. We run to the end of the alleyway. Vinnie steps in front and holds his hands up, ordering us to stop "Fuld take your Parka off, you, take off your Harrington, we need to look like kids, not Mods", snaps Vinnie, as he takes off his flight jacket. "Vinnie, let's stroll to my house, 10 minutes max, mum and dad are out, we can hide there until it's over, anyway your bike is there." Fuld and Vinnie nod in agreement.

My house is a stone's throw away, right across Sidney Road, down Montague Close and hey presto The Egmont estate. My head tells me once we get to Montague Close, we are there. So pleased Ginger wasn't there, as he would have recognised me and Vinnie for sure, at least this way we can have an alibi, think things out. This feels like the Great Escape, trying to avoid the Nazis and make it to the Swiss border. The walk down Churchfield Road seems like a life time, every car that passes us from behind makes us hold our breath, but we can't hear the sound of footsteps or running. From the distance we still hear the screams and shouts of the wedding party, it may not have been the best day of their lives, but we have certainly made it the most interesting.

We get to Montague Close with ease, just another two or three minutes and we are safe. I fumble in my Sta Press, bypass my Italian leather wallet, present from my father, and feel my trusted key ring, house key and padlock key, plus some odd keys I added to make it look more important. I like it when I go round Tom's or Rick's and put my wallet and keys on the table, all part of the Mod thing, little details that go beyond a Parka and a pair of Hush Puppies. We've done it, another great escape, and another Mod legend for the kids at Crutchfield and school. I hear a car turn down Montague Close, the car is slowly coming beside us, can't be the Old Bill, it would be 'Screaming' Sirens' and all that, but it's going a little too slow to sound like someone just driving home. Vinnie, Fuld and me look at each other sideways "Don't turn round, keep walking" orders Vinnie. I am not going to disagree, reckon it's nerves and when the car passes we will all have a laugh. Slowly it comes to our side, fuck, I see the colour navy blue, the start of a white border with the letters I,C E, then we all see the driver, it's fucking PC 'Ginger' Macdonald with some ape like policeman in the passenger seat, looking like the cat that had got the cream.

"Afternoon, let me give you a lift home, there are some yobos about, ain't safe for such young kids like you." I fall to my knees, he really is a bastard.

IX

A Light Breeze

It's the last day of school tomorrow and the summer holiday begins, I can't wait, I just can't. Me and the boys will be in the 3rd year, well it's actually called the 4th Year as Rydens doesn't have a 1st year, you go straight into the 2nd year when you start. I forgot to say that at the Start! (Any excuse to quote The Jam), I just didn't think it was that important. Next term I am down for all CSE's, not too bothered, I am sure I will find something after school. It isn't that I am not clever, far from it, got very bad handwriting though and trouble with spelling, slow, sometimes, but not thick enough to get special teaching, so easier for the teachers just to say I am no good, I hate them all.

But I've got a good feeling it's going to be a good year, as we won't be the new kids any fucking more, in fact we will be top of the tree. The final year at Rydens is called the 5th year, they've all gone, done their exams and all pissed off into the real world, tea boy jobs, college or signing on...... my turn in about a year's time, what am I going to do after school? Start a Mod church spreading the gospel, I don't know, not really thinking about it. Here's a poem I wrote about school, The School Gate,

Outside the school gate
The real world waits
Teachers won't tell us of our fate

Just to eat the school dinner off our plate
The Kids at school
Aren't no fools,
We won't follow your rules
Trying to make us feel small

Written loads over the last two years, might show you a few, not sure yet. Weller and Page got me into writing, also some mad punk poet called John Cooper Clarke. BBC 2 had this new programme called Something Else, first one in 1979 had The Jam, Joy Division and this crazy guy with this mad hair going down the escalator at some train station, going on about the Bloody Train always being Bloody Late, my mouth hit the floor, went out and bought a pad, well my mother did on the Monday, and been writing ever since, just got round to showing you.

At Rydens we have a field big enough for about 5 football pitches, we go there for a smoke and a lark about. Anyway some of the main lads from the 4th year who, by default, are now the top year, saw us lot having a fag and all that and decided to run us, big mistake. They didn't reckon on Rydens' very own punk rocker, Stone, and soul boy extraordinaire Curtis the Cat. Great lad, loves his football, call him the Cat, 'cos he looks like a cat. Goes to Chelsea with his brothers and a few of his mates, tells us about the punch ups at the football, he loves it, in fact lives it. Well, these two led the charge back, Stone at the front, head down, charging like a rhino, with Curtis slightly behind giving us orders, in fact he kept shouting out "Stand, Stand."

I loved it, we were united, the tough kids of our year broke away and went for them, those who'd thought they were the toughs of the 4th year, a few punches and kicks and they ran, fucking ran, we gave chase right up to the main building, we stopped once they got to the entrance and hid inside. Stone turned to us all and screamed, a loud tribal scream, every muscle in his body was clenched, veins in his neck showing, like a scene from Planet of The Apes, we started screaming back and jumping up and down, we all knew that as that chick said in Grease, we "rule the school," our fucking Year top dogs, no more bullying, us, united…. Fucking yes.

That was the first bit of fun I've had in ages. Been grounded since my arrest, bike under lock and key again, so I've been walking to and from school which means I have to get up earlier and arrive home later, so I miss a few good TV shows. Yet got to know a lot of the boys better, as many like to walk and we like to nick from the shops down the Halfway, or annoy the odd motorist, and sometimes, well a lot, I walk back to Susie's, she lives near Walton Station, we walk hand in hand, I feel loved and wanted. Her mother, Pauline, who actually likes me believe it or not, was a Mod in the sixties, saw The Small Faces, The Action and even The Beatles. Sometimes I am lying on Susie's bed, she puts some music on and dances, she's smiling, so happy and she don't care if I am watching, "It's all too beautiful" as The Small Faces once sung.

I forget about school, even being a Mod, not interested in trouble or what clothes to wear, it's just me and her and the music, we do other things as well, but that's between me and my sweetheart. Then once I am away from her I become the mad Mod again, I am so confused, but fuck it, I am young. Haven't seen much of Vinnie, he's grounded as well, not allowed to use his bike, we speak on the phone, he sounded bored, and he's on report at school, like me, which means you have to behave. Love to have a big mansion with Susie when I am older and Vinnie living next door, just wishful thinking of a school boy I suppose.

My parents and Vinnie's have actually become friends after our arrest, they know we are good mates but thought it would be better to 'have a break', fuck it, makes it sound like we are married. But as for Tom's mother and father they think it was us that led their son astray. My father phoned them and told them straight that it was him that followed us at his own free will.

Listen to this, Tom is a thief, he works at the newsagent, you know where I first met PC MacDonald, he's nicking money out of the till, cigarettes and sweets, but he looks so innocent, like "butter wouldn't melt in his mouth" as my mother would say. I am not going to tell tales but it does annoy me that his parents think he is the golden boy. I am not banned from Tom's house, which is good as it has a side extension; it's a big room with a huge record player. We, as in me, Rick and Tom practice our dancing there, mainly to sixties stuff, Motown and Stax, look at the photos and the write ups in Richard Barnes Mods! book, like the Shake, The Monkey and we just make a few up. Rick is a good dancer, but always faces the corner, tells me "the secret of being a good dancer is that no one can truly see you dance." I have no idea what he means by this, but it sounds good. Since I've been banned from going out, haven't been to Crutchfield, but heard of the kids now going to the Walton Hop. Heard the Old Bill are giving any Mod looking kid a hard time, but mark my words we will be back.

Back to the arrest, it was total chaos at the cop shop, young teenager Mods and wedding guests brawling and having to be kept apart. I gazed at Vinnie as he was wrestling with some overweight uncle from the wedding, he looked so happy, he ain't right in the head, but I love him for that. The cells and interview rooms were all full. I was interviewed in an office, had to wait a while as my mother and father were in Southend for the day, got back about 5, the police kept trying to get hold of them. I was hoping they would let me out and could come back with them later, as that is what they did with Vinnie, his mother and father were away, not sure where, so they let him go and he had to come back later with them, jammy bastard, that's Vinnie's luck all over.

Ginger kept telling me that the others had grassed on me. I've watched The Sweeney too many times to know his game, wanker, fucking wanker. He kept this going until my father turned up, my mother wouldn't come down, too ashamed. After my interview I was released on police bail pending further inquiries. It wasn't as simple as that, I was far from calm, yet I didn't name names, just said I was walking along saw an army of Mods being chased and I followed them. The pub men and the wedding guests didn't know us by name, so how could they name names. The charge over my head was ABH, Affray and Criminal Damage. I shitted myself, as that would mean a visit to Feltham Borstal. I had to wait and waiting was the most horrible part

Anyway I can relax, all charges have been dropped. The Dennis Waterman look alike from the pub men, whose real name is Charles Vroom, didn't want the embarrassment of admitting he took a beating from some teenagers. The Wedding Party didn't want to press charges, as neither did the Mods. I think Snowy knew a few of the guests, had a word with them and had a word with us, the police went mad. But two from the Wedding Party were charged with disrupting the peace, as were a couple of the Mods, nothing heavy, a fine for the adults and a warning for my lot as it's their first offence. Sadly Mint was charged with ABH and Robbery, not his first offence, so looks like he will stand trial before one for Fulham.

Now for the big one, the shop window. Well, if you remember, Harris jumped through on his own accord, he was trying to drop kick us, but no one pushed him. Witnesses came forward to say what he did, we didn't, none of the Mods did. Harris may be an enemy but I would rather side with Harris than the Old Bill any day. He was charged with Criminal Damage, however, Vinnie's dad Theo, who owns the local Greek Restaurant, paid for the window to be replaced, must be some sort of honour among local Restaurant owners. The local paper, The Surrey Herald, had a photo of him with the fish and chip shop owners, with bleeding Vinnie in a wonderful three button suit, standing in front of the new window with the headline about local businessman helps another business. After that Theo's restaurant was fully booked every night so he got his money back. My father reckons he did it for the publicity and also put it in his tax return, crafty, just like his son.

So the fish and chip shop owners, pleased with their new and even better shop window, decided to drop the charges and business boomed for them. Word got back to the other witnesses who Harris was, so they didn't come forward. As for Harris, he just got a few grazes and according to Tom, ain't got no problem with us, as no one grassed. Harris went into Tom's newsagent to get some fags and was even laughing about it. As for Dennis Waterman AKA Charlie, don't know, not sure if there will be any more problems with him, but I do think he will think twice. I couldn't believe my luck, only found out at the start of the week, the final week of school, summer here we come. My mother was so relieved she has given me some money to meet Vinnie after school, so we can have a Wimpy and a good catch up, even better he's staying over.

Rydens doesn't have a nearby school so the end of year tradition is to have a fight with the shop keepers from the Halfway on the Halfway Green, been going for over 10 years. The shopkeepers are just as much up for it as we are, in fact I heard it was their idea, last year's was a blinder. Brought Hersham Road to a standstill, running battles, a few windows went through, the police hate it as do our teachers. But we were in the 3rd year and weren't allowed to join in, just watch. It's only 20 per year from the next 4th and 5th years, 40 of us vs 40 of the shop keepers, a lot of them are their mates, those are the rules. Stone did ask me, he knows I am not tough like him, but he knows I love madness, the mini riot saw to that, but I wanted to see Vinnie, plus I had just got let off by the police. Stone told me he can't wait and wants to do George the Fishmonger. I was genuinely upset I couldn't make it, Curtis the Cat said there's always next year.

So the riot has done me the world of good in terms of being accepted, the kids at school think I am totally insane, I really like that. We have won the respect of the older Walton Mods and The Virgin Soldiers. Susie tells all her friends about me and my friend's mad adventures, she likes the madness too, deep down. Even made The Surrey Herald, two weeks in a row, first week a report of the riot and second week readers letters, some hating us, some supporting us, one geezer said we should be hanged, that made my day. The 'Walton Puppy Mods' are now part of local and Mod folklore, who says crime doesn't pay, it fucking does if you don't get caught or charged.

I race home, throw my school clothes on the bedroom floor, change, go for the real casual look, light jeans, white crew neck tee shirt with dark blue boating shoes, lovely hot day, cola float, cheese burger and fries with my best mate Vinnie. Like me, Vinnie is so proud that we are now part of Mod legends, beating up the Pub Men, fighting the police in the church, how the story has grown with all the facts twisted, I really like that.

As it's a nice day, we cycle to the river after our Wimpy. Walton has a nice river, tow paths, woods, there we are sitting by the river, just like when we met two summers ago, total and utter strangers, now the best of friends, it's going to be a good summer holiday. We are laughing, talking about the clothes we want, well Vinnie talks about the Lambretta or the Vespa he wants, I talk about The Beatles and Motown, Vinnie loves Motown. It's so nice, then the magic is broken "Two little gay Mods looking for somewhere to bum each other." I look round, as does Vinnie, its Pemberton, still dressing like a Skinhead from 1979, holding a can of special brew – wanker

Pemberton, the brute, the thug, the fool, left Rydens about a year or so ago, seen him walking round town a few times, he certainly ain't 'the boy about town.' He's given us the odd wanker sign or two finger accompanied with abuse, usually about beating us up or bumming us or both, he is seriously ill, he needs help, he needs locking up. All he wants to do, or so it seems, is to cause aggro, usually on kids smaller and younger than him. It's a beautiful summer's day, and all he wants to do is to cause trouble, why? I seriously can't understand it.

My father once told me bullies are the loneliest and most confused people in the world, well I am not going to feel sorry for him. Pemberton is like a supervillain from Batman, different henchmen and a moll with him in each new story. What gets me is that the birds who are always with him are so good looking, oozing with sex appeal. They must love his 'hard man' image, and it is an image, as no one has ever seen him fight someone his own age or size. This is the first time in yonks I am face to face with him. I am nervous, real scared, but experience has taught me not to show fear. I look at Vinnie, my word he has put on some muscles.

"So who bums who, you or you, or do you take turns, I want to see ya bum each other, show me your arses, I want to see ya suck each pencil dick."

"Leave us alone mate, I'll get Snowy" snaps Vinnie

"He ain't here."

"Yeah, but he'll find ya." I decide to join in, after our little battle with Dennis Waterman and Luke Hazard I enjoy standing my ground. Pemberton laughs, "Like it, got a bit of bottle, heard about your fight with Charlie, four on one, well there's three of us, come on get your cocks out and start wanking." I am dumbfounded, he seems more interested in our penises and arses than hitting us "Hit them Paul" croaks one of his cronies, "Nay, not yet, I want to see your cocks, your small little cocks, I want to see you wank, hic" he's drunk, totally and utterly pissed.

"Leave them alone Paul, they're just kids" pipes up a busty blonde with a flick in white frilly blouse, which works well with her curves. Pemberton turns round to face busty blondie, who could pass easily as Dolly Parton's sister "Shut it girl or you'll get my belt." Dolly shakes her head, and sighs, Pemberton walks or staggers forward towards her, and he reaches out and pulls the back of her hair, "Don't give me any lip woman." I look at Vinnie; both his fists are clenched, oh well, all for nothing and all that, if he goes in, so do I. Dolly screams, pulls away from his grip, leaving a lot of her hair in Pemberton's dirty hand. She faces him and pulls her leg back and bang, straight in the goolies, just like Purdy from the New Avengers, now that's a real English Rose, Joanna Lumley, every boy in Nursery Road Middle School wanted to marry her. She's certainly got power, as our arch enemy hits the floor screaming in pain, one of his henchmen steps forward to hit her, he pulls her arm back leaving his face wide open, she lashes out with her right hand, fingers pointing and her sharp nails showing, scratches him all the way down his face, she's fucking Catwoman.

He screams, she pulls her hand back and blood is pouring down his face, the other Skinhead throws his can of beer, oh yeah, all three were drinking apart from the bird, who started off as Dolly

Parton, then turned into Purdy before becoming Catwoman. The stupid idiot forgot that Vinnie is about a foot away from him and moving forward, pow, my best mate lamps him the perfect punch, he falls to the floor. Vinnie has really become tough and fearless. I feel useless as I didn't contribute to this, but not wishing to feel left out, I ran to Pemberton and I kick him when he's down. "Come on" shouts Vinnie, we run with Catwoman as fast as we can back to our bikes. "I'll give you a ride", says Vinnie to the Catwoman, fuck it, he has beaten me to it. Vinnie stands whilst he rides; she wraps her arms round his waist as we ride off on the river dirt track towards a pub called The Anglers. I get to the side of Vinnie and Catwoman, he turns sideways and gives me that cheeky wink.

We get to the pub, it's closed, so we sit on the tables outside. Catwoman gets her fags out, I happily take one but Vinnie doesn't, he hates smoking. "I was going to dump him, he ain't got a job, lives with his mother, she spoils him, stupid cow, always drunk on my bleeding money, picks on kids like you."

"But what about him getting you?"

"Sweetheart, I'm Sharon Butler."

"Pleased to meet ya."

Ha, you must know my brothers Tom, Darren, Stuart and me baby brother George." I smile, they are well known travellers from around here who settled at Field Common, a council estate near Rydens, been there a few times, it's alright. I've heard the Butlers can handle themselves, not bullies. George, the youngest, is in my year at school, he's alright, really good at football, plays for the team, we ain't mates, but we chat, big Arsenal supporter, not sure what music he likes, dresses smart, bit like an old man though. Eventually the pub opens, she buys us a coke each, I did ask for a beer. But she just giggled, she uses the phone box and soon a few of her mates come down, wonderful looking girls who all doted on Vinnie, said I was cute but they adored him. Then a few boys turned up, and we were edged out, in fact they stopped talking to us, the novelty must have worn off, so we ride back to my house, I need a nap.

"If I could get away with killing Pemberton, I would. We need revenge, fucked off with him, we need to teach him a lesson," states Vinnie as he is lying on my bed face down, leaving me, me in my own bedroom, sitting on the floor cross legged.

"Comfortable?"

"It's OK, could do with another pillow." I pull one of my pillows out from under his head, and lightly hit him on his back "Vinnie, the Butlers will have a word, or we could get Snowy or the Virgin Soldiers. Sharon knocked him out."

Vinnie pulled himself up and slams both his feet on the floor, which gets my mother shouting up the stairs to be quiet. I shout it's Vinnie, to which she replies I am not to lie and he's our guest, to which he gives his Cheshire Cat grin. "But that's it, it's other people fighting our battles, we need to fight for ourselves." Vinnie seems hell bent on revenge, it's rare, in fact extremely rare for Vinnie to be this serious, but it seems he's had enough of being a Puppy Mod in the eyes of others. His desire and 'time for action', inspires and intrigues me, we exchange usual ideas, none seem that great, then I tell him about Mr Bates and the day I went into his house. Vinnie's jaw drops, puts both his arms out and pulls me forward and kisses me on my forehand.

" I knew you were a little devil like me and now I've seen your dark side come out." I feel like I am sharing my bedroom with Darth Vader. Vinnie is right, I've been naughty at school, a rebel maybe, but not as dark as I used to be, I mean I broke into Bates' house on my own and for fun, no mates to impress. I've been too occupied with fitting in, now to have some fun, not Mod fun, but mad fun.

We wait a few weeks for the dust to settle with Pemberton. We need a base, as luck would have it my mother and father have gone to Italy for a week, I think they wanted a break from us and left my brother in charge, which is OK he's got his Mrs over, they are either in his bedroom or out in London. I can't wait when I am a little bit older to have nights out in London. Mod clubs and Mod gigs. I shall miss going on holiday to Italy with my parents but

I am too old now to go with them. Pemberton, the bastard, lives down a road called Charlton Road, which is close to me, too close for my liking. The houses were built before the Second World War, neat and tidy, not slums, like I would expect him to live in. He lives with just his mother, heard his father fucked off when he was a nipper. I found all about him and where he lived by helping a Soul Boy mate out, Niven, as in David, but Neil is his first name, poor bastard, Neil Niven what a name.

He's a nice lad, chubby, likes his funk music, played me nice records and obsessed with Page 3. When his old man chucks out The Sun, he cuts out Page 3, has loads, thousands of them under his bed, can't stop talking about it. I help him with his Informer round and he helps me. When I have seen Pemberton I have always ducked. It was Niven that pointed out his mother, nice looking woman for her age, seems down trodden and works at the bakers at the top of Terrace Road, a stone's throw from my house and Pemberton's. Heard that he got a job labouring, in fact saw him, luckily he didn't see me but he was covered in shit, he looked knackered as he walked home.

With Pemberton living so close, Vinnie and I decide to walk to his house with our paperboy bags, I've got two of them, one for my Informer round and the other for the newsagent. I am still doing an early morning paper round, but not much to really tell, other than I walk around and put papers through people's letter boxes, don't go for madness, just want it over and done with. We've got black gloves in the bags and wearing shoes too big for us, Vinnie came up with the idea having the shoes too big for us, for footprints, I think his father gave him the advice. We nicked them from Oxfam, this shoplifting is getting out of control, but I love the excitement of putting some up your jumper, in your pocket and strolling out of the shop.

We casually walk down the driveway by the side of his house, leading to two back gates, his and the neighbours. I start to whistle, thinking it will help us not to look suspicious, but as I can't whistle for toffees it doesn't have the desired effect. Vinnie gives an odd look, walks over and whispers in my ear "You might as well be wearing a mask and a bag with SWAG written across the side," I quietly chuckle but shut up.

Much to our delight and surprise the back gate was unlocked, I could have climbed over, but this makes our life much easier. His garden is well kept, and quite tranquil, nice flowers, a shed and an oak tree at the back with a little table and chairs, I seriously can't picture Pemberton sitting here and enjoying afternoon tea. There are fir trees by the fences, this is good, as it blocks out anyone looking in. After admiring his garden we head to the back door, to the left is the kitchen window, no windows are open.

"Before we smash anything, let's look for a back door key, I reckon his mother leaves it out for him as he's too thick to have a key." Good suggestion by Vinnie as it seems the back gate is kept unlocked deliberately for when he comes home pissed or after work. After looking under a few garden items outside I find it underneath a brick by the side of the house near the kitchen window. Took us five minutes to find, either they are really trusting or stupid, I am going for stupid. We put our gloves on and enter the house, Vinnie sends me back to wipe my prints off the brick, as I am doing this I am wondering why he isn't doing it.

His house is rather tidy too, a lot of china and brass, common as my mother would call it, a picture of the Queen, he even has a video player. Nice settee and clean shag pile carpet, the kitchen is well kept too, his mum has a microwave. My mum said we are getting one soon, heats up food in seconds. Like professional burglars, not that I know how they act other than what I've read in comics, books or seen in films, we walk around in total silence, and only speaking in whispers or the use of our hands. We head towards the stairs to find his bedroom; I must say this is exciting.

Upstairs is the same as downstairs, clean bathroom, his mother's room is tidy but looks like a museum piece, with this old bed, in fact it's a bit creepy, I keep thinking Lizzie Borden, the bird who killed her father and step mother with an axe, fuck that. We find a small room full of boxes, perfectly stacked whilst gathering dust, then we find the room we have been searching for, well it was easy to find in an old fashioned 2 up 2 down, well in this case 3 up and 2 down in a semi-detached house, hardly a mansion. Pemberton's bedroom, nothing on the door, but we open it, there's a large swastika flag draped over a cupboard in the right hand corner facing the bed, on the wall next to his bed is a poster of Adolf Hitler, what a wanker and on the wall opposite loads, I mean loads, of photos of Skinheads, some cut out of magazines and newspapers, some of his own photos, and by his bed on the floor are a few copies of Tintin, The Red Sea Sharks, read that, Tintin in Tibet, read that, The Broken Ear, read that, in fact read all of the Tintin books, he also has a few Famous Five books by his bedside, never read any of them, we start laughing at his reading matter.

After the laughter stops Vinnie looks at the wall and whispers "No photos of any birds", he's right, no photos of the girlfriends or posters of Debbie Harry or such like. "Maybe he's got a stash of dirty magazines under the bed?" I say.

"Have a look and I will have a look in his wardrobe," suggests Vinnie.

I slowly go on my knees to examine the contents under the bed, I see two tatty and beaten up cardboard boxes, bent at the corners as if Pemberton pulls them out a lot, so I do the same. Not much dust on them, so he gets the boxes out a lot. I've been reading Sherlock Holmes and watching Basil Rathbone as Holmes, which has helped me with my skills of deduction, oh yeah, for a while, really got into Alfred Hitchcock and The Three Investigators, no shame there, but just don't talk about it to my Mod friends.

I look up to see Vinnie pulling Pemberton's clothes out slowly, takes out a really nice bright red Fred Perry, holds it against his chest, seems to fit him perfectly and puts it in the paperboy bag. I return to the boxes, open the first one, just some old NMEs, Sounds, underneath them some glossy magazines, I pull one out, on the cover is a fella totally starkers with a huge cock, I toss it to one side, and pull out some more magazines, all the same. Then go for the other box, same as the first one, music papers on the top and underneath dirty mags with photos of men. Looking at the words and the names of the magazines, it ain't English, flick through them, and putting them down, as this ain't turning me on, I find many of the pages sticking together, Pemberton must love reading these. That's it, I can't look at them anymore. I hear "He's a fucking poof" I look up, Vinnie is standing over my shoulder with his mouth wide open.

"No wonder he kept going on about bumming you, he really wanted to, he fancies you," jokes Vinnie, then I have this vision of me dressed up like a little girl sitting next to Pemberton in the Wimpy. I ran to the toilet to be sick, as I do I hear Vinnie laughing. All this time Pemberton really wanted to bum me. Of all the people in Walton to fancy me the most, it's him, I return to the bedroom, Vinnie has pulled out all the mags, "find some scissors, glue or pritt stick and a pen, oh and a bin bag, we'll take home some of his grub."

Finding household items isn't hard, especially with someone who is a basic thinker like Pemberton's mother, bin bag and scissors, found two pairs in the kitchen drawers, pen and glue in a cupboard in the living room. Vinnie came down the stairs as I was just about to walk up he takes one pair of scissors and "cut these photos out and stick them all over the place, I am going to cut the right sleeve off of every shirt and Fred Perry top, he's got and the right leg of every pair of jeans and Sta Press."

That's what I did whilst Vinnie destroys his clothes, I glue them all over the walls in the hallway, bathroom, kitchen, mum's room. I ain't going to go into detail about these mags, use your imagination; I didn't enjoy cutting the photos out but loved sticking them on the wall.

As we are leaving, Vinnie pulls down some painting of a horse and cart in some field, leaving a clean space on the living room wall, then he writes in big black letters, YOU FUCKIN POOF, ALL WILL KNOW SOON! Then we nick all his food, or the food we like, burgers, sausages, baked beans, oven ready chips and a large bottle of Heinz Ketchup, put them in the bin bag which we put into my paperboy bags and walk out like nothing has happened. But it has, we have exposed Pemberton, now we have to wait for the retaliation, but we will be ready.......

X

Desolation Row

There hasn't been any repercussion from Pemberton, as he's disappeared, pissed off without a trace, and no one, apart from Vinnie and me obviously, know what has happened. We have beaten and humiliated Pemberton, not via brute force but using our minds, pure fucking 100 per cent Mod.

I am at home during the summer holiday, got the radio on, Capital Radio, fuck knows why, perhaps I can't be bothered to put some records on. They're playing hits from a few years back, Vienna by Ultravox comes on. Hated that song back then and hate it even more so now. The phone rings so I do the bleeding obvious and answer it.

It's Tom "Hello…. is that Vienna, you've got on?

"Fuck off it's the radio." I slam the phone down and turn off the radio in annoyance. The phone rings five minute later, it's Tom again "Listen I won't tell anyone about you listening to Ultravox, it will be our little secret"

"You're too kind Tom" he does get on my nerves sometimes

"Mate, guess what?" He's phoned me for a guessing game.

"I have no idea, what."

"Come on guess?"

"You're a poof, but I knew that already."

"You're the only bum bandit around here."

I am really not in the mood to exchange homosexual insults, especially after discovering the truth about Pemberton.

"I give up Tom", he really is boring me

"You're going to love it" he certainly Keeps Me Hanging On, sorry couldn't resist quoting a Motown song.

"I seriously can't guess mate."

"I tell ya, you are going to love it."

I must say, he does sound excited, my mind starts ticking. "OK, let me think, it's got to be something to do with …. Mod."

"You're getting warm."

Mod, that doesn't really narrow down my options, so many things to think about, my brain starts ticking there is one thing that Tom and I both love, and that's The Jam.

"The Jam?"

"Bingo!" Tom now has my full attention.

"Tell me more." Fuck I am starting to sound like the chorus from Grease doing Summer Nights.

"Mate, I have found out where The Jam rehearse in Woking, fancy a trip down there? We can tell them we are local Mods, starting a fanzine, sure Weller and the others will give us an interview."

"Let's do it, see ya."

"See ya."

I put the phone down with a huge beaming smile, fuck, The Jam.

That evening we, as in Rick and Vinnie too, have no idea why Vinnie tagged along as he hates The Jam, all meet round Tom's to discuss a plan of action to meet Woking's finest. But Tom being Tom, didn't keep his word and told the others that he caught me listening to Vienna, we had an argument that lasted about an hour. Rick believing me, that it was the radio, whilst Vinnie siding with Tom, I knew he would. In the end, it ended like it does when I have a disagreement with Tom - a fight.

Rick and Vinnie stepped back and cheered us on, only to be broken when his father came into the extension to find Tom and me rolling about the floor. My friendship with Tom is very odd, as we do seem to love to fight each other, very strange. Anyway after the aggro, we hatch a plan.

Even though Woking is a 15 minute train journey, four short stops from Walton-on-Thames, it's the first time we've ever paid a pilgrimage to the hometown of The Jam, and getting off at the station I can totally understand why, it's a shithole, grey, built up, yet giving a sense of a country village. On the train, we couldn't help but sing Jam songs, apart from Vinnie. He still can't stand The Jam as you know, and is only here for something to do as he gets bored on his own.

I've borrowed my brother's cassette player, new batteries, new tape and a mike. Rick has brought along his brother's camera, but won't let anyone touch it. Vinnie has brought nothing whilst Tom brought a Mod fanzine for an English project or something as proof that we do a fanzine. It does look good, it's a bit of a rip off of *Extraordinary Sensations* and an earlier fanzine, *Direction, Reaction, Creation.* I really hate to say this and trust me, I do, but Tom is a good writer, could easily see him getting a job at the NME or Melody Maker.

Whilst I know what I want to say but my spelling and grammar are shit. I wish they would invent a machine that can check spelling and grammar. I keep watching Tomorrow's World hoping to see one. They've invented a fucking machine that plays Snooker called Hissing Sid, what good is all that? And a synthesiser that can sample real sounds, hate synths and their music, it's all that New Romantics shit, Depeche Mode and crap like that, there is no soul there. I want to hear loud guitars, angry and passionate well-dressed geezers, sexy black women singing. Rick reckons sampling will be massive, I can't see it myself, sample music, what's the point, make your own, that's what I say. Anyway Tom, Rick and I have agreed, if we get the interview with Paul or Bruce or Rick, or all three, then we will start a fanzine, please don't get me started on what the title will be, we've agreed to discuss that when or if we get the interview.

The rehearsal room is in a village called Horsell, a bus ride from Woking. As you know, we love The Jam and love knowing everything about them, we know they have this minder, a big geezer called Ken Walker who could easily pass off as the brother of Giant Haystacks, the wrestler, a great big lump, must weigh around 20 stone, about 7 feet tall, a big fat face, long dirty greasy hair and a long beard to match. Seen Walker at The Jam's gigs I've been to, pulling off some young Mod when they jump on stage to dance to The Jam. I nearly did it myself, but when I saw him I thought best not. By all accounts you have to get past him to get to the band.

That's why I think Vinnie came along, he loves getting in places he shouldn't, using his charm, wit and imagination. As you can imagine, we've all dressed up. Rick is simple, blue jeans, white tennis top and hush puppies, with a lovely green flight jacket. Tom, red and white boating blazer, white sta press, bowling shoes. Vinnie, black Brutus button down shirt, jeans and boating shoes, and a Fred Perry jacket, which used to be his uncle Sid's. Me, grey sta press, white button down shirt, (from Marks and Spencer, but looks good), my new blue bowling shoes and borrowed my brother's new Levis jacket which I hid this morning. Heard him looking for it, and my mother suggested he might have left it round Tracey's, that's his girlfriend. My brother may not be a Mod anymore, but sometimes does buy the odd piece of Mod clothing, which is good for me.

My brother was a Mod for a while after watching Quadrophenia and then stopped. I don't see Mod as a fashion and as the film Quadrophenia says, "It's a Way of Life". I still haven't seen the film. Three fucking times we've tried, twice at Esher cinema, ending up watching the extended version of Close Encounters one time and the other time some shit American comedy, forget the title, as I was too upset because I didn't get to see the film I really wanted to watch. Also tried one time in the London's West End. Got no further than the ticket office. I am pleased to say that Rick and Tom haven't seen the Quadrophenia film either, would hate it if Tom had seen it, we fight non-stop over this. Vinnie's Uncle

Sid in the East End, oh yeah at any given opportunity Vinnie will go on about his tough London family. Anyway Sid has a bootleg which Vinnie has watched, but Sid wouldn't lend it to him, saying "fuck off Vinnie, you will do copies. Forget your Uncle Sid and get yourself a scooter". Even though Vinnie goes on about his relatives I do find it interesting that a lot of them are ex Mods or villains. Most on my mum's side are from the East End and Essex but seem to have been more on the rocker's side, and got jobs as opposed to helping out The Krays and doing a bit of smash and grab. I suppose criminality is in Vinnie's blood, as he is a great shop lifter, loves to nick bikes and all that. I can see him becoming a gangster in a few years, moving back to the East End. Me, I don't know what I am going to do, a pop star or a writer, who knows.

I am always on edge in a new town. We managed to get to the bus stop without any problems, didn't see any Skinheads, a few ordinary looking kids, and one Mod, smartly dressed, maybe a bit older than us, he nodded and smiled, and we smiled back, even Vinnie. The bus ride was only 15 minutes, full of old ladies, it didn't take long before we were out of the horrible town centre and entered into the English countryside, beautiful, really beautiful. Tom had a map of where the rehearsal room was and last night he got his dad to drive there so he could find it easily today. Since the departure of Mott, don't miss him and found him quite dull to be honest. Tom thinks he is the leader, as did Mott, and like Mott, he isn't and never will be. But Tom wanted to be the one that got us to the rehearsal room. His dad did offer us a lift, said he would take the morning off work, Tom thankfully said no as there was no way we were going to try and meet The Jam by turning up in a car with one of our parents. Still cringe when I think about Rick's mother dropping us off at the Guildford Civic.

We get off the bus in Horsell, a real English village; you could easily see a murder taking place here like in Agatha Christie's books, just has that feel to it. Tom, Rick, Vinnie and I are feeling nervous yet excited, we stop at a baker's for a drink and a bacon sandwich. I don't have one as I am too agitated to eat, no appetite,

I am moments away from meeting The Jam, Paul, Bruce and Rick, the band that has guided and inspired me. Vinnie paid for the drinks and food, I didn't even have a coffee, just a coke, as my mouth is so dry.

Nice of Vinnie to pay, as he wanted to show off the twenty pound note that his father gave him this morning. The old lady behind the counter couldn't believe a 14 year old boy has so much money, even I felt the same 'cos Rick and I feel rich with a fiver. Tom thinks he's a playboy with his tenner, stolen from the till at work I have to add. Vinnie loves to show off, to me that makes him a good Mod, "If you've got it, flaunt it", remember seeing Zero Mostel saying that in a film, *The Producers*, watched with my father and my brother one Friday night, funny, laughed so much I couldn't sleep after watching it.

After having our late breakfast or early lunch, but does it really matter? We march like a small army following Tom, who is holding the map like a general going into war. Tom makes a point of stepping ahead, he loves the power, little does he know me and Vinnie are pulling faces behind his back. We follow 'our leader' into a country lane with no houses either side, the lane leads us towards what looks like an old farm building. Forgot to say, if you're wondering how we found this out, Tom's elder sister is going out with someone from Polydor, the label The Jam are with and he told Tom's sister about this rehearsal room and how The Jam use it, who told Tom, who quite clearly told us. As we approach old Macdonald's farm we hear a guitar tuning up, and someone playing the drums, fucking hell it's Paul and Rick warming up. We quicken up our pace, looking round we can see no other Mods, this will be wonderful, us and The Jam, our own private little gig, and even better the door is open. No longer able to contain ourselves we run, even Vinnie, to the rehearsal room. The guitar is now playing, sounds a little different to what I would expect from Weller, and the drums start to get a rhythm going, I am in total heaven, so happy, so excited. What a great way to meet The Jam in person, seeing them rehearse two feet away from you. Heard from loads of Mods I've met they are really nice to their fans, let them in for sound checks and even into the studio sometimes.

We get into the main entrance, which is open, it's very run down, a dirty kitchen right in front of us, a cage full of heavy boxes, and a few guitars and amps, two large black doors, one is firmly shut and the one to the left, where the music is coming from, is slightly open. We all look at each other, even Vinnie looks happy, he knows meeting The Jam will do good for his Mod credentials. Taking a deep breath, I step in front of Tom, this is my moment. The Jam changed my life, I found them, I wasn't influenced by anyone. Tom tries to push back, I give him a slight elbow in the stomach and push open the door. I want Paul and Rick to see me leading this group. I walk into the rehearsal room and my mouth drops to the floor.

Standing before us are two fucking head bangers, the drummer is wearing an AC/DC tee–shirt whilst the guitarist is just wearing a leather jacket, with jeans, they look at us, look at each other and start laughing. "It's The Mods" says the drummer, then they go into a slightly rock instrumental version of The Merton Parkas' You Need Wheels, which I must say, doesn't sound bad. After about 2 to 3 minutes of this musical interlude they stop and I eventually reply "And you're not The Jam", which makes them hysterical. The drummer gets out from behind his kit and faces us. "What the fuck makes you think The Jam are here?" Vinnie, Rick and I all look at Tom, his faces goes red, what an idiot.

"We heard they rehearse here?"

The head bangers start laughing, "Oh, they don't, but I do know why you might think that, we are old mates with Bruce."

I find this hard to believe that Bruce would be friends with head bangers. "He pops in every now and then for a chat. He's having his house decorated, left some of his basses here, so they don't get paint on them." That's nice to know but I look at Tom with a real snarl on my face, he looks straight down at the floor.

The head bangers look at us with some pity " Sorry, listen you're welcome to hang about, but got two rock bands coming down, looking at ya, ain't no thing mate;" I smile, as do the others, "Thanks mate, but we best go." I look at Vinnie, who is unusually quiet, I keep expecting him to be cheeky. We say goodbye, the head bangers even give us a couple of fags, and offer us a beer, but none of us were in the mood for a drink. We close the door behind us and head to the main entrance. "I'll catch you up, I need to use the toilet" says Vinnie, none of us pay much attention, other than a disgruntled sound. I feel so sad, so low; I thought this was my destiny, I barge past Tom as I make my way out, he doesn't retaliate. We start walking up the lane, Vinnie seems to be taking his time, perhaps he's having a shit, then I heard a panting sound, look over and see him carrying a huge black guitar case, he stops, puts it down and turns it sideways, there in huge white letters are the words Bruce Foxton... fuck me.

"You've got to take it back" demands Tom, as we sit in the woodland nearby. The case is open wide, furry inside and there before us, is Foxton's trade mark black Rickenbacker bass guitar. I feel like we have discovered the Holy Grail. We are just looking, not touching it's far too beautiful and magical too. Rick says he fancies learning to play the bass, told ya his brother Steve plays the bass, got some good records. Steve played me and Rick this new British funk band called Level 42, like the sound, their bass player, who is the main singer is called Mark King, his style is called slap bass, very punchy and moves with the drum, like it a lot. Yet Rick and I haven't told our other Mod friends about our new love for Level 42. I hope Rick gets good on the bass as I need to get better on the guitar. I could see Vinnie on the drums, just like Keith Moon and Tom with his blonde hair as the lead singer, we could be the new Who, with me, like Pete Townsend writing the songs not Tom, I would fucking hate that.

Vinnie is shaking his head and laughing at Tom. "Listen Tom, phone The Jam's record label". "Polydor" I butt in.

Thanks, yea, Polydor tell them we've got the bass and does what's his name, Foxy something still want it back? Arrange to meet them, bring our tape player and camera, you at least get to meet the Fox and you'll get your interview, everyone will love it, you've conned The Jam" Tom smiles and replies "Good idea". I really love it.

We get back to Woking with ease, no run-ins with any kids and all that and get back to Walton just after lunch. Vinnie walks over to the phone box to call his dad for a lift, as Tom, Rick and I guard the bass thinking what a great way to meet the Jam.

Tom is an amazing negotiator, I hate to say that as you know. He managed to get through to some fella called Dennis Munday at Polydor Records, apparently he helps out with The Jam's record sales. According to Tom, Dennis seems a nice guy, was laughing at our prank and assured us Bruce would find it funny too. We arranged to go back to the farm where we stole the bass this coming Saturday. After hearing the news, we had to put on The Jam and play them at full blast. Vinnie you are ingenious, four young fans who 'conned' The Jam. I bet we get our photo taken by the NME or Sounds, or maybe The Face, us four school boys handing the bass back to Bruce, and having a laugh. Hope Paul and Rick are there, I'm off to prepare my wardrobe.

Getting to the farm this time was easier, as we knew the way, we were on a mission, Woking was busier than before, and I was pleased to get on the bus. Don't like the town centre, reminds of The Jam's song *Dream Time*. Even Vinnie is thrilled, word got around, and loads of the Mods, from our gang and the older lot wanted in. No, this one is for us, we will be the faces of the Walton Mods and beyond. Tom, Rick, Vinnie and I all look immaculate, though I am not going to bore you with details.

As we walk down the lane we see Bruce Foxton, my God, it's Bruce, fucking Bruce Foxton, and with him is the Giant Haystacks look alike, Ken Walker, and another messy geezer, but there's no sign of Paul or Rick, oh well, one member of The Jam, nice. Bruce looks rather annoyed, and starts pointing at us as we approach, we give him a little wave, but he doesn't smile nor wave back, instead Ken Walker walks over to us, this is starting to feel a bit tense.

"OK, who nicked the bass?"

Me, Rick and Tom all look at Vinnie with no prompting as he was holding the bass, which he insisted he did.

"Alright you come here, the rest of you muppets stay there," and with this, the other minder walks forward towards us. We all exchange glances, as Vinnie walks off like a man going to the gallows.

The other minder holds his arms up and stops us from moving forward, but he doesn't block our view, we see Bruce aggressively grab the bass off Vinnie and walk off into the farm building, Vinnie looks back at us scared, I have never seen him that afraid before. Then Ken Walker faces Vinnie pulls his arm and smack straight into his stomach, Vinnie falls to his knees clutching his gut the moment Walker's fist lands on his stomach. I am totally and utterly speechless, I can't laugh, I can't shout, I can't cry. "Come on" shouts Walker to the other minder, who for some reason, gives Tom a big shove who falls straight to the ground. As the other minder is walking towards Walker, Vinnie gets up, looking rather dishevelled with head down slowly strolls towards us. As their paths cross the other minder moves to Vinnie's left and gives him a shoulder charge, Vinnie looks up and simply says "fuck off" and carries on walking, the other minder smiles and heads into the farm building.

Tom, Rick and I are all in shock as he joins us. One of my heroes minder just winded my best friend that is something no kid should see. Vinnie doesn't look his perky self, he just shakes his head and quietly mutters to himself "Well he certainly ain't no Paul McCartney, I bet he would have found it funny."

We didn't speak the rest of the journey home, got called a wanker by a couple of very scruffy looking Skinheads, but after finding out Pemberton was a poof they really don't scare me anymore. In fact they backed off when Vinnie turned to face them, he was in the mood for a fight. Skinheads look so fucking dated now, I mean how the fuck can you expand on Jeans, DM Boots, Braces and Fred Perry, you fucking can't. I am seeing less and less Skinheads around these days, a lot of kids seem to be going Soul

Boy, grey sta press, slip-on black shoes and one button leather box jackets, seen a few kids wearing tennis tops that aren't Fred Perry, I quite like the colours.

When we got back to Walton later, none of us wanted to hang about, so I go home, usually got the house to myself at the weekend, father and mother like to go out, visit friends, relatives and my brother is either working or round his girlfriend's in Kingston. I like being on my own sometimes, nice to read, listen to music, watch TV, have a round of toast. Before we set off home Vinnie asked us not to tell anyone about this - so we've all promised

Don't think Tom will have enthusiasm for doing a fanzine after this mad day, perhaps I might start working on a modern poetry one. As you know I'm a huge fan of John Cooper Clarke and another poet called Dave Waller. At the end of *In The City* song book, The Jam's debut album in case you didn't know, it has some poems by Dave Waller, a mate of Paul Weller's and he used to be in The Jam. His poems touched and inspired me, then I went and bought his book *Notes From Hostile Street*, had to order and wait for it from WH Smith as it came out a few years ago.

I am hoping to write 10 good poems and send them to Weller, as I heard he might be bringing a book out with new poets like Dave Waller. It feels like Paul Weller want us, as in the fans, to do our own thing, a 'youth explosion', and that's what we are, a mighty bang with parkas on. Also love reading Ian Page's words, they inspire me, must have read the Glory Boys lyrics so many times, even copied New Dance from the album out for my English homework, got 7 out of 10, with a few comments from Mr Scot, the English teacher. I think Weller's, Clarke's and Page's words should be taught at school for English. They mean more to me and other kids than Shakespeare. I seriously don't understand it, watched a few Shakespearian plays on BBC 2, couldn't understand a word. My brother was in Romeo and Juliet played Paris, who got murdered, it was quite good fun seeing your own brother getting stabbed on stage, I jumped up and cheered, only to be told to shut up by my mother who shook her head in shame.

As for life in Walton and me, well Crutchfield Lane has closed down, but we weren't going there anymore, I think I said that. Apparently the Vicar got sectioned, don't know why or how, and no one has taken it over. Rick and I are talking about going down to The Walton Hop, they don't play Motown, The Jam, Stax or anything Mod related as I told you, Jazz Funk and modern soul mainly. Might give it a whirl, heard there's a Mod thing for kids our age at Le Beat Route, reckon that is more like it. We should be going into London more, as a Mod I need to move around. Saving up for a pair of suede Chelsea boots, will look great with my white sta press, seen a few Mods wearing psychedelic shirts, paisley patterns, like that look, even I am growing my hair a bit longer, want one of the sixties type sailing hats or maybe might start wearing a beret, saw a cracking photo of Weller with one. Love all this moving clothes around, trying out new things. Love the fact that Tom and Rick are always changing their look, Vinnie doesn't so much, but he always looks smart. We dress the best, compared to our other Mod friends, most don't seem to think further than a parka and a pair of hush puppies, perhaps we are faces. I am going to wear eye liner, fancy it, no I ain't like Pemberton, but I know the original Mods used to. My God, would love to go back to the sixties, go shopping down Carnaby Street, then go and watch The Small Faces at The Marquee then a dance down Ham Yard, dressed in a tailor made Italian suit, riding an SX Lambretta, black, with a beautiful shapely brunette on the back, with my own pad, near Baker Street, just like Sherlock Holmes. Oh well, maybe one day, as the two paper rounds and my allowance, don't call it pocket money anymore, certainly ain't going to pay for it.

Haven't been in the town centre for a couple of Saturday's, weather has been shit. Vinnie hasn't really been any fun since the Foxton incident, seen Rick and Tom, they ain't that bothered about the town centre at the moment, they seem to be doing a lot of homework. I don't, I hate it, I hate school I think you know that. I can understand why that school girl in America shot all those teachers dead one Monday morning in the late summer of 1979. The Boomtown Rats, an Irish band a sort of a mixture between punk and new wave band, wrote a song about it, more or less straight after it happened called *I Don't Like Mondays,* 'cos apparently that's what she said when asked why she had done it. The song got to Number 1. I quite liked it and can relate to the lyrics.

Anyway, my mother asked me to pop down to Safeway's to pick up some things, told her I might stop by the Wimpy, she didn't look too pleased. But I did and saw a couple of the Mods I know, said hello to them then went and got my mother some butter and milk as she had asked. As I am leaving the supermarket I drop them 'cos standing right before my eyes, is the mad man himself, Mr Bates. Again dressed like Christie, and looking just as evil, he looks at me, no he glares at me, just like Christopher Lee does when he's Dracula, and he utters a sinister sounding "hello." Arghhh I ran out of the shop.

Life had been on the up so much, with so many twists and turns, I had forgotten about him, thought he would never see the light of day again, I was wrong. I will have to tell my mother the shops were closed or they had run out, as seeing Mr Bates reminds me there is a life outside of Mod, and it can be bad.

XI

Leave it Out

Mr Bates' contorted face is pure evil, each snarl displays hatred and the blood vessels in the whites of his eyes demonstrate anger. I feel like I am face to face with evil itself. I am trembling, never trembled like this before in my life, but I can hardly move as he has me tied to a table in some posh kitchen, face up in just my underpants and parka, there's some Beethoven music playing in the background. The kitchen is vast with many cupboards and old copper pots and pans, old fashioned, like you would see in a Hammer horror film. I don't like it here, all I want to do is go home, just to be at home safe and happy.

I knew Mr Bates was a nutter, easy pickings for a wind up, but I didn't think that he was this so totally and utterly insane. All I did was to draw moustaches on his photos of the Queen but that was 3 years ago. OK, he did go to prison because of it, but it wasn't me swinging a shovel about, smashing windows, and he tried to hang Peter and Betty, why? 'Cos he can't take a joke, "Jesus" as Vinnie would say.

What makes this even stranger, is that Mr Bates is dressed like the Queen but without the crown and with an old fashioned flat cap instead. It's the outfit Her Majesty wears on special occasions when she parades outside Buckingham Palace in the horse and carriage, as she did for the Silver Jubilee and for Charles and

Diana's wedding, now Diana I like, she's gorgeous. But that isn't enough, Mr Bates is wearing this bright red lipstick, really bright.

So you get the picture. After I ran out of Safeway's, he chased me. I thought I had lost him but alas no, as I was walking towards my front door, he jumped on me from behind and covered my mouth with a cloth which must have been soaked in chloroform, I passed out in seconds. Seen chloroform used loads of times in films, but I never thought in a million years it would happen to me. Once I came round, I found myself here with this psycho dressed like ER bending over me with the face of a lunatic, and behind him is a collection of scalps in a cloth bag, just like the ones Jack the Ripper or Mr Hyde would use. But he hasn't touched them, instead he just keeps looking at me, then moves to the kitchen sink where there is a pot of tea and scones, cream ones as well. I have no appetite, I am too frightened but anyway he doesn't offer me one. Mr Bates is sipping his tea and eating the scones with delightful manners, no crumbs or anything.

"What gives you the right to enter into people's houses and destroy their property? Hmmm? Ruin items they have worked for, bought and treasured, I knew it was you, I always did, but I could never prove it... you give me a good answer I will make your death quick and painless, give me a bad answer, I will make your death slow and painful" says Mr Bates in a high pitched and crackling voice just like The Wicked Witch of the West from The Wizard Of Oz, which plays havoc with my ear drums.

I reply "What about if I give an OK answer, do I live Mr Bates?" I can't believe I just said that, what am I thinking?

"Typical cheek of the youth of today, you never fought in a war to obtain your freedom". "My father reckons you never fought in the war, the army rejected you 'cos of your flat feet". "Silence! I don't have flat feet" with this he slaps me across the face, the pain stings and then it sinks in that I am going to die, that this is the last thing I will see in my life, a man dressed like Elizabeth II about to skin me alive. I wanted so much out of life, I wanted to form a band, write a book, marry Susie my sunshine girl.

I wanted to travel the world, buy the best clothes a Mod could buy, meet Paul Weller, John Cooper Clarke, Ian Page, see fucking Quadrophenia. I will die a Mod never having seen that film. God is cruel, he is really cruel. I am going to miss my mother, my father, my brother. Vinnie, oh Vinnie, my mad and wonderful friend, the fun we have had. Rick, you wonderful tortured artist you inspire me so much and Tom, oh Tom I know we argue and fight, but I do love you, you have opened my eyes to so much

All the boys and girls from school, the Mods, all of them, I will never hear The Jam again and see them become bigger than The Beatles. Why did I do what I did, why did I cross that line, perhaps if I beg he will forgive me, and let me live. "Mr Bates, I am truly sorry, I really am, please don't kill me, I don't want to die, I am too young, I have friends, family and a beautiful girlfriend, my Susie." "She is a whore!" he says. I might be dead soon, but I will die fighting for the honour of her name. "You don't even know her!"

"I know her kind."

"What the fuck do you mean you know her kind? She's just a teenager, a well behaved one too."

"Well, she hangs out with yobbos, Mods, silly boys dressed up in silly clothes, listening to silly music. No, not like the church, where we learn about the values of life and the creation of life itself."

He is really starting to annoy me now with the shit coming out of his mouth.

"Fuck off Mr Bates, name one war started in the name of fashion or music, most wars are in the name of religion or to steal some land, greed. We want to educate and inspire people, you want to control people, fuck you and your church."

Mr Bates is silent, he seems to pause for a second, he goes to speak, but is lost for words, really lost, he scratches his head, then he falls to his knees, and begins to sob. My word, I might be able to persuade him to let me go. I might have turned this around.

"Bernard, is it OK if I call you Bernard."

"Yes" he whimpers, "It's OK."

"Look, just let me go, I promise to go to church, help the community out, give up Mod and become a good Christian."

He looks at me with such sad eyes then the madness returns and he leaps up, "You are the son of Satan, a devil's child, you hurt school teachers who want to help you, policemen who want to protect you, shop keepers who want to serve you, other teenagers who belong to no tribe who want to befriend you, pub men who.....want......."

"Who want to do what? Go on then, what do they want to do to us?"

He's lost for words, the others he had a fair point I will admit that, but as for the pub men they just want to bully us.

"OK fair point, I will take them off the list, but you break into people's homes and vandalise them, sending the occupants mad and it's not just me. You did it to a nice young man misunderstood by society, he just wanted to be your friend, remember Paul Pemberton.....you destroyed him."

How the hell did he know about that, has he been following me all this time?.

"Paul" he yells out, the kitchen door opens and fuck it, it's Pemberton dressed up like a beefeater, you know the chaps that guard the Tower of London, I have seen it all now. Pemberton nods at Mr Bates, who nods back; my death is going to be slow and painful I can feel it. Then the kitchen door opens again, in comes a gorilla dressed like a butler holding a silver tray with a china tea set and some more scones.

"Your tea and scones Sir Bates" says the gorilla in a very posh voice. Hold on, the gorilla just spoke, what the hell is going on. Then I hear a voice "wake up luv", a beautiful heavenly voice sent to save me, my eyes start to open.

I blink and look up and see Susie with her long curly dark hair and bright blue eyes looking down at me. I catch my breath, pull myself up and find myself on the sofa in her front room. I turn my head and see her mother sitting at the dining table chuckling. I am alive, I am alive, it was a nightmare, I am alive. Thank you

God. I take it back about you being cruel, heat of the moment, I hope you understand. I remember now, I helped Susie's father out today with the gardening to earn some money for clothes for my next trip to Carnaby Street. It was the hardest day's work I've ever done in my life, in fact the first day's work I have ever done in my life. After breaking out into a sweat and aching all over it convinces me even more to become a pop star, a writer or an actor, as I certainly don't want to be a gardener. I must have fallen asleep straight after as I have never felt so tired before. To be honest I think I just collapsed on the sofa. I reach out and hold her hand, pull her towards me, lightly kiss her cheek, it feels so good to touch something so beautiful. "Stop it" she giggles "You'll embarrass me in front of mum, anyway get washed up and changed, Father is taking us out for an Indian." I am speechless, touched and happy, not a big fan of curry but this one will taste so nice.

"You look so happy, never seen you so happy, you're always trying to look miserable like Paul Weller," jokes Susie.

Just happy to be alive Susie, thinking about changing things, maybe stop being a Mod, maybe do something else." OK I know, throughout I've been going on about being a Mod for life, but I am confused, really confused, I mean is it worth all this aggro, I don't know, all this worrying about what I look like, what music to listen to, what places to go to, I loved it but I don't know, maybe the dream I had was my subconscious telling me stop this.

"Luv you are the best Mod out of all your lot, you live and breathe it." I smile, when I am with Susie there are no arrests, madness, fights or arguments, I feel the most happiness ever, yet I get drawn into the trouble, the mischief, the mayhem. I want to be loved and also I want to be mad. Her mother, Pauline, smiles at me, she always does, she never talks down to me or questions what I am doing, not like all the other adults I know. She allows me to breathe and Susie's father, Harold, a successful builder, has taken to me. Of late I've been coming here a lot over the summer holidays, they even let me stay in the guest room. I love waking in the morning, walking downstairs and having breakfast with them, then her father drops me off home. I get in and whack on The Who or The Jam, go see Tom and Rick. Then Mod, Mod, Mod, I can't take it anymore, I really can't, perhaps I need a holiday.

After the Indian, Susie's parents drop me off as they are all going away tomorrow, Hastings or somewhere. They are getting up early so I couldn't stay, but I don't mind going home. I enter my house and announce to my family I am no longer a Mod, I have no interest in it anymore, I want to be a normal teenager. My brother and father burst out laughing, and my mother goes on about how much she's spent on clothes for me over the last two years. I was hoping for a bit more support. I go to my room, look at the clothes I have that are non-Mod and start to read anything that isn't fucking Mod related.

I have been cut off from all the other Mods, well Vinnie was shocked, but we are still friends. Rick seemed upset though we are still friends, and Tom said I was never a Mod to begin with, so I punched him straight in the mouth, I'd had enough and he punched me back, so we had another fight, I won't miss that anymore. Most of the time I am reading, new authors I had never heard of before, like Jack London, Oscar Wilde, Albert Camus, Franz Kafka, Hunters S Thompson, Ray Bradbury. Susie lent me the books, her mother is a big reader, think she studied English in the 60s in London. She has passed down her knowledge to her daughter who has passed it onto her boyfriend, me. I like that, ideas being passed from one generation to another. Pauline said the books would appeal to me and they do, beautiful outsiders seeing the world in a different light, like The Jam or Secret Affair, shit I'm going all Mod again! From reading these authors I feel quite inspired. I dress very sensibly now and often get shouted at by other Mods as I walk through Walton, but I don't care, I really don't. I asked my mother and father if I could move to Susie's but they said no, I thought they would be glad to see the back of me. Yet my mother adores Susie, and out of all my friends they get on the best. I like it when Susie is round, and she and my mother have a chat, I get a warm feeling inside. School starts soon, what I thought would be a summer of madness, hasn't happened. When I am not seeing Susie, I see some of the rough boys like Rash, but it's just chatting and hanging out. Susie and I are off shopping tomorrow, to London, her father and mother are coming with us, but they will let us wander on our own. I am looking forward to that, both of us have money to spend.

Here I am in Carnaby Street, don't know how I came to be here, but it felt like instinct, Harold and Pauline are somewhere or other, but we've agreed to meet at Bar Italia in about an hour. Forgotten I've been there before with my father, he used to work in Covent Garden and took me there. I see all these Mods, I feel drawn to them, like I should be with them. I look at Susie dressed in a nice pink summer dress with a beret so lovely, she looks at me and sweetly smiles. I love her so much, yet I do miss being here with Tom, Rick and Vinnie. "I'll back in a minute luv, just wait here, I am going to look at something." She kisses my cheek and walks off, I turn and face a shop window, I see my reflection, I am a normal teenager, but I don't like it, it's not me, I want to be different, fight authority, find solace with Weller, I am lost in my own world, then there's a tap on my shoulder, it's Susie holding a Shelley's bag, I open it, it's those black Chelsea boots I have been after.

"You're a Mod luv. I love your passion for it, don't change, I might not be here forever, but you can't change your passion". Tears roll down my cheeks, I smile and head towards Robot. Ten minutes later I am standing in front of the same shop window, this time in a white and cream paisley shirt, light blue hipster trousers and my new Chelsea boots, the clothes I wore are now in the bin.   I am reborn, I am a Mod again. I take Susie's beret lightly off her head and put it on mine. "Sweetie, can I borrow your eyeliner?" She shakes her head and giggles as she always does and passes it to me, I outline my eyes, thick, really thick, I step back and check myself once again. The blood rushes through my veins, my heart is pumping, this what I am. I am a Mod, a true Mod, I lost my way for three fucking weeks, but maybe I needed to step out to see where I belong.

Fuck you Mr Bates, I will destroy your house again, fuck you Pemberton you fucking poof, fuck you Chicken George ramming your shit down our throats, in fact fuck all of you. Well apart from our parents who don't get Mod but we do love them anyway. I need Mod, I want it, the music, clothes, madness, aggro and pure passion, it's intense, but I need that, it's my drug. I want to see Weller give it some, hear Steve Marriott sing, hear the sound of a scooter in chrome come bombing down the road - it is My World. I turn to face the street, the Mods walk past and nod at me, I am back, I am truly back, Susie pulls me towards her, kisses my lips, steps back and says "Beautiful". Yes I am, a beautiful mad Mod.

It's a week to go before school, and it has taken about three days for the Mods to accept me back, I have to say I am pleasantly surprised. It was more or less overnight, suppose it was my new look and new found confidence. Tom and I had a cry, followed by a big hug, Vinnie is happy to see me "back where I rightfully belong", his words, which I thought were very nice, in fact I was close to tears when he said that to me. I am off to see Rick as no one has seen him for a few weeks, spoke to him briefly on the phone, but he said he was busy. I said with what, he wouldn't go into detail, so I am off to pay him a surprise visit.

Susie said she knew I would become a Mod again, and she deliberately took me to Carnaby Street so that I "could find myself again". Also she said she would have dumped me if I had stayed a normal teenager, she said it's my madness, my mind, the Mod in me and my amazing good looks, well she didn't actually say the bit about the amazing good looks, but I think she would have said that, you do believe me don't ya? Anyway it's all these things that attract her to me. She also said I couldn't be the boyfriend whose only friend is his girlfriend, she also loves to go out with Tina, Michelle and Liz and says I need to hang out with Vinnie, Tom and Rick.

Having read loads before I became a Mod again, I am going to write this book called A Surreal Teenager's Dream, about a kid in a tower block and his crazy world, but that's as far as I have got, well come on, I've only just thought about it. But I want Rick to do the illustrations so that's another reason why I am going round there. I am concerned that he hasn't shown his face for a few weeks, he's different, but he's always there, I miss seeing him.

I ring the doorbell, no answer, so I ring again, this time keeping my finger on the bell, it seems to be going on forever before I hear a voice above my head "Take your finger off the bell, you're giving me earache."

I look up and see a familiar and friendly face, but he looks troubled, maybe not troubled but different, also he seems to have no shirt on.

What do you want?" he asks.

"A cheese sandwich Rick."

"Fuck off," he smiles, five minutes later I am in his kitchen, drinking coffee and eating a nice cheese and onion sandwich, nothing odd about this, however he's in his underpants covered in paint and hasn't explained why he's looking like this.

"What's this look Rick? Mod Pop art in underpants?"

"Nay, abstract soul with a bang."

Like it. "So what have you been doing, no one has heard from you."

"Busy."

"Busy walking about in your underpants and painting yourself, oh yeah Susie's mate Tina fancies you."

He looks up, it's true she does and she's a good looking girl. A lot of girls like Rick, he is handsome and confident. Telling him about Tina makes him more open, as he takes me to his bedroom, telling me he has something to show me, no… not like that!

There before me, is this painting that should be in a huge art gallery in London or Paris or somewhere like that. It's a painting of these Mods marching towards Big Ben, real sixties Mod in sharp suits with pretty Modettes, real attention to detail you can even see the cufflinks on the shirts and buttons on the jackets. I knew he was good, but I didn't know he was this good. I fall to my knees, it is the most beautiful painting I have seen. I want it, I want to show it to the world, I look at Rick with total amazement.

"I couldn't come out, got up one morning, started painting, couldn't stop, had to finish it, which I did an hour before you knocked."

"Didn't you get lonely?" I ask.

"If you want to create you have to cut yourself off, do you think Paul Weller writes his songs between food shopping and going down the pub?"

Good advice, and now I understand why he is semi-naked. "Do you paint in your underpants for the ease?" I ask.

"No, I put them on just as you knocked", I feel a bit sick with a mental image of him painting naked.

Rick has ventured out with me, Vinnie and good old Christopher. As we stand in the queue for The Walton Hop, we are dressed Mod, but not overly as we are entering into unknown territory, full of the usual enemies of the Mods. Yes it's Saturday night, we can't hang round the town centre anymore, that is so bloody boring, how many fags can you smoke, how many mean-ingless chats can you have, how many times can you spit on the pavement? Also our parents are so bored with us hanging round each other's houses, we ain't allowed up London on a Saturday night, also we don't have the money to do that, and most of the places won't let us in. And as you know Crutchfield is no more, so The Hop it is.

The Walton Hop has dropped the age to 16 upwards, heard they let anyone in who has reached puberty. The reason is, up until a few months ago, loads of 18 year olds upwards went to the Walton Hop every Friday and Saturday religiously, then it dawned on them they could actually go to the pubs, get in a car and go anywhere they wanted, get on a train, get into London and go to a club, plus the Hop doesn't sell booze. So they stopped coming, that's the intelligence of the kids round here, took them fucking years to realise there is more to life than the Hop when you hit 18. So, almost overnight, they stopped coming, the dance floor was empty, dropped the Friday night and lowered the age as there is no alcohol being sold.

Me, I am looking forward to it. Susie is going with her friends, so I will at least get a goodnight kiss. I've been listening to Jazz funk and Modern soul, as you know, I like it, I really do, but let's keep that our little secret. I can see so much of Mod in the music, soul, blues, jazz all given a modern day treatment. As we approach, an older looking skinhead is standing there, but he seems friendly and greets us, 'the kids', and behind him is this huge old Teddy Boy, a cross between John Weller and Kenny Walker, he looks like he is in command and makes everyone stand in line, so he can pat us down. It's a half-hearted attempt, as loads of the kids smuggle in small bottles of vodka and stuff like that. I'm not that bothered, I like beer, in fact I love beer, but not spirits, the smell of it makes me sick. Christopher has a small bottle of vodka, no doubt it will help attract the ladies, not that he needs to. Tom is away this weekend with his family, gone to Portsmouth, got an uncle there. So Vinnie and me, before we met the others, went round Tom's house, got a pitch fork and a shovel out of his father's garden shed, and dug up all the back garden. I really should see a psychiatrist, I really should, and so should Vinnie.

As I walk in, just like when I went to Crutchfield for the first time, I was overwhelmed by the dancing... kids my age and a bit older moving with such attitude - it's tribal, it's appealing. I recognise some familiar faces and see my best friend from school, Rash, my black brother. He is doing what he does best, dancing and smiling. I gaze in his direction and nod with a smile, we are too old to wave so now nodding and winking is what we do instead, he nods back with his laid back attitude. Then I see my beautiful sunshine girl, I wink and blow her a kiss, she returns the gesture. I look at her, just looking, she glances back with a smile. I break from my trance and see Vinnie already kissing Liz Vince, she is a good looking girl and if I weren't with Susie I'd wish I was in Vinnie's place, but please don't tell my girlfriend.

Oh yeah, The Hop is like an old village hall, but bigger with a horrible wooden floor and a large stage, dirty white walls, with an odd looking DJ (yes I know the term now) sitting in a booth by the side of the stage. I look at him, he looks seedy, something I don't like or trust, he's looks too old to be here, I don't like it. There are disco lights and an old cinema screen, a small one above the DJ, showing films, really old soft porn, oh yeah, we've watched a few, but I am sure it would bore you senseless and might even make my words illegal if I told ya about what we watch round Tom's, when his parents are out. But I will tell you this, Tom has built up the muscles on his right wrist, I am sure you understand what I mean.

I get the sense I am being watched, not by kids my age but the men behind the booth, they keep looking at me, and one smiles at me. After my recent experience with Pemberton fear is no longer in my soul. I gaze back with a slight snarl, he puts his head down and turns to the other men and seems to whisper something, they all look away. I failed to realise Vinnie was standing by my side doing the same, and boy, he does look tough. "Coke bar?" he suggests and I follow him.

Loads of kids well dressed, not Mod, but well dressed, Soul boys and girls are drinking coke and eating crisps in the bar. I got loads of hello's as most of them go to Rydens. Vickie Anderson, who is a year older than me, goes mad when she sees Christopher, who also followed us into the coke bar, really mad, I am used to it. The coke bar is round the back, along with the cloak room and stairs to the balcony, and toilets - not much here really, but it's the people.

You've seen the film Grease, of course you have, and the High School dance with all the chairs on the side and all the ugly kids sitting there, well that's what it is like at the Hop, except that some beautiful kids sit there. I have my coke and cheese & onion crisps and go back into the hall, absorbing everything, I detach myself from the crowd, the music is strong, the dancing is getting madder, I am tapping my feet, I need to dance. This song comes on, it is fast and funky, I hear something about not wanting a fascist groove thing, like it, see the kids sing along to it, I get up and dance, I am loving it, really loving it. I exchange glances with the others, catch Susie's eye who smiles and slightly laughs, I turn and see Vinnie doing the usual circling his index finger round his head to say that I am mad, but I seriously don't care.

The rest of the evening was good fun, no fights, even bumped into Mickey Davies from Nursery Road, who told me that everyone back in Sunbury calls me the King of the Walton Mods, not sure if he was joking, but good to see him, after all this time. We all walked home, Vinnie was staying at mine, and Christopher was getting picked up from mine with Rick, who danced all night long, he looked so good. Rick lives near me, I think you know that. The only trouble we nearly had was at the newly opened Kentucky Fried Chicken. We bumped into our old friends, the pub men. A new lot, never seen them before, we got our chicken and fries to take back to mine, my mother is good, she's happy for me and my friends to sit round the kitchen table to eat our food. Well one of the pub men went straight to Vinnie and tried to steal his food, Vinnie just knocked him out, one punch, bang... his mates, or so called mates ran off, we gave slight chase, but were more interested in eating our chicken.

The whole family has been invited to Theo's Greek restaurant in Oatlands Village for Sunday dinner. Vinnie isn't there, gone out with Liz Vince. Oatlands is a nice small compact type village between Weybridge and Walton. I like it here, all the houses look like they could be haunted, told my mother that, she says I watch too many horror films. The meal is lovely, all on the house, Vinnie's dad, Theo, a real charmer, keeps coming over giving my father and mother more wine, they didn't drive and caught a taxi instead. I am happy, it's going so well, no school tomorrow, but back to school soon, shit. Then my father looks up and shouts out "bastard!"

I look over my shoulder and oh shit, there's a signed photo of Charlie Cairoli on the wall. My father starts screaming and shouting, Theo comes over "What's wrong?" "That man, that bastard, the worst clown to ever grace this earth, you know him Theo?"

"Yeah, he used to come to my restaurant in North London, always a laugh when Charlie came in."

"Come again?" Theo looks perplexed at my father's reply.

"Sorry, Charlie was good fun, always made us laugh, isn't that right Lillie?"

Lillie is Vinnie's mother, who is by the door saying good bye to all the customers as it is now 10.00ish.

"What's that Theo?"

"You liked Charlie didn't you?"

Lillie smiles and seems to recall a fond memory and replies "Charlie was a laugh, a real scream". These words send my father apoplectic.

"A real scream, a real fucking scream, I'll give you a real scream", and with this, he stands up, turns round and picks up his chair, oh no, he's not, he raises it above his head and throws it straight at the main window, which smashes into pieces. The other customers in the restaurant are silent, dumbfounded, my mother hangs her head in shame, my brother looks embarrassed, while I am simply amused.

My father turns to Theo and Lillie, who are struck speechless "Now, that's a real fucking scream"

XII

A Crafty Cigarette

Luckily for my father Theo did not press charges for criminal damage. Later my mother explained to him about my father's problem with Charlie Cairoli. Theo, being the wise man that he is, totally understood and told my mother that he was once in The Kinks for a brief time, as 2nd guitar and backing vocals. They did a gig in Acton, this was before they made it big, by the way. Theo broke his strings during a song and Ray Davies never called him again, or so he told my mother. Now Theo can't listen to any records by The Kinks and has to leave the room the moment their music comes on. Shit, both Vinnie's father and my father could have been huge stars, that's quite depressing.

After my father smashed the window, he was wrestled to the floor by the two chefs and three waiters. Theo and Lillie were too stunned to move. I have to say that my father did put up a good fight with the staff, but once he was overpowered he was taken to Theo's office at the back and he calmed down. My father, of course, paid for the window and apologised to Theo, Lillie and the rest of the staff. He is now seeing a psychiatrist on a weekly basis to get over his anger issues about Charlie Cairoli and clowns in general, as it has been an issue for many years. If a clown comes on the TV he will scream and shout at it. Once we saw a clown walking through Richmond, why, I have no idea but we were in the car, a Fiat, and my father tried to mount the pavement and run him over, if it hadn't been for my mother grabbing hold of the steering wheel, my father may have been sent to prison for murder.

We aren't allowed any books or comics that contain anything to do with clowns, as it can send my father insane, I am not joking. Over the years I have hidden my Batman comics that feature any stories with The Joker, I am telling you that would send my father into total psycho mode. I am sure with help he will overcome his issues with Charlie Cairoli and clowns. The worst incident I do remember was many years back, before I was a Mod and living in Sunbury. Billy Smart's Circus with a funfair came to town, well Hampton Court which is very near Sunbury.

My uncle, my father's brother Franco was over on holiday. My mother drove, so my father and my uncle could have a drink, we got there early afternoon just as the pubs were opening. My mother, my brother and me walked round the fair whilst my father and my uncle went over the road to a nearby pub. We went on a few rides and an hour or so later they both came back rather drunk, and wanted to go to the circus. My father reassured my mother he was fine and wouldn't have any problems with the clowns, it took a while but eventually she gave in with a little persuasion from me and my brother, along with my uncle, because he wanted to go to the circus too. We got in, it was brilliant, the lion tamer, trapeze artistes, a man being fired out of a cannon... I loved it. I was a happy child, then the sodding clowns came on, driving into the ring in a battered car, three of them, the car fell apart, the clowns fell out of the car and the whole of the audience roared with laughter, apart from one man, my father. My mother and I looked at him, I could see the hatred in his eyes, and before long he got up, making towards the ring screaming at the clowns. My mother shouted at him to come back, whilst my uncle had passed out, my brother hung his head in shame, and I just wanted to see a fight. I really did and egged my father on, only to be told to shut up by my mother.

The clowns stood together ready for it, my father went in

swinging, he landed a good punch on one clown, a small tubby bloke with a really big red nose, he went straight down. The whole audience again roared with laughter, in fact they were pissing themselves laughing, it was hilarious. Then the other two larger clowns laid into my father, he went down, face down, the other clown got up and then all three of them started to kick my father hard with those clown shoes, again all this time the audience thought this was part of the act and were loving it. Then it dawned on me, no child, and that is what I was at the time, should witness this, their father being beaten up by a gang of circus clowns in the middle of the ring. I started to cry, my mother was weeping and my brother was in bits. Eventually the ringmaster, along with the bearded lady, the lion tamer and the World's strongest man, managed to drag the clowns off him. They offered us complimentary tickets, which I wanted to accept but my mother turned them down. We took my father to Ashford Hospital where he was treated for minor cuts and bruises, and it was taken no further, but me, I was scarred for life with this memory of our family's evening at the circus.

First day back at school, new year, new look and new attitude, turned up this morning, light blue Levi's denim jacket, with my school shirt, button down of course, black sta press trousers, beret and eye liner. Walked in with total confidence, and not one of the rough boys said a word, in fact they seemed to respect my bravery. I am now the best Mod at Rydens, Mott is still one and a lot of other kids have become Mods since when I started, but not one will dare wear what I wore today.   Two years it's taken me, and now I am more than accepted, I am admired, all the tough ones from the rough boys speak to me, we have a laugh, I join in, wind up the teachers, tease other kids, I don't bully, just tease. But all of us feel a new strength and power, two years ago we were small scruffy kids, now we have filled out, we're better dressed and much tougher, "boy... it's a tough, tough world and you've got to be tough in it," to make our mark and show the teachers and the year above that we mean business.

Curtis the Cat got us to block the entrance of the dining room chanting "We shall not, we shall not be moved". A few teachers waded in to break it up which resulted in a scuffle, and got me a detention first day, good, fuck them, so what if I am half an hour late home. I want me and the rough boys to have our presence felt. The teachers have picked on us too long and I am not going to start singing Pink Floyd's Another Brick in The Wall, "Hey Teacher Leave Us Kids Alone", fucking progressive rock shit, written by some dope smoking hippies in some fucking mansion in the South of France, fuck off, we are the kids and we don't want your help.

During the summer, my brother made me stay up two Sundays in a row to watch two films; Unman, Wittering & Zigo and IF. In Unman, Wittering & Zigo the kids are murderers and bully a new teacher and his wife and in IF they shoot the teachers at the end. I loved the films, even took notes and at the end of IF, I kissed my brother on the forehead, which I haven't done since I was a child... again he has inspired me. OK, these were set in public schools, a million miles away from Rydens, but what they had, which we don't, is leadership and organisation. Straight away I thought of Stone, Rash and Curtis the Cat, and me of course, a Mod, a Punk, a black kid and a Soul boy, the Kids are united.

Second week back at school I arrange to meet them in the toilet, no, we ain't poofs. Lofty Jones, one of Curtis' mates, keeps watch outside. Lofty is a bit thick but good at fighting. I feel like we are planning the great escape, tell them about the films, how they planned their attacks and we need leadership. Curtis had also seen Unman, Wittering & Zigo and IF, and liked the idea, so did Rash, and Stone got so excited he head butted one of the toilet doors and broke it. That passion was good to see. I put myself forward as leader, but Stone said he wanted to be the leader. I wasn't going to argue and with him in charge, all the rough boys will follow and listen. Stone is a man in a boy's body. For his 11th birthday, his dad, uncles, cousins and brother took him pub fighting, apparently it's a family tradition whilst most of us either go to the cinema, the Wimpy, London Zoo or whatever with friends for our birthday, his family were teaching him how to pub brawl.

He took to it like a duck takes to water. I do like Stone, he's a total loon, I like loons a lot. After hatching our plan, I have lunch with Susie, I try to sing to her All or Nothing, she puts her fingers in her ears and says I ain't no Steve Marriott. Then I walk home alone, I want to be on my own.

After talking to Rick I now understand the importance of being alone, yet my "tranquillity of solitude" is shattered when I see Mr Bates walking through Walton Town Centre. He sees me, doesn't even smile or wave, just glares, makes me shiver, he looks evil, really evil. I wouldn't be surprised if he becomes the Surrey Ripper, just like they had in Yorkshire. He was arrested at the start of the year, The Yorkshire Ripper - some chap called Peter Sutcliffe, he has evil eyes just like Mr Bates.

I get in, listen to some music, into Motown again, and I read a bit, enjoying this American author, Hunter S Thompson, a bit barmy, hard to understand but I like it. He hates the American dream, and takes the piss out of it. Don't bother watching TV, only seem to watch it if there is something on that I want to watch, which isn't that often. I call Vinnie, have a chat, then walk round to see Rick, have a coffee and a cheese sandwich, he loves his cheese sandwiches, and then I call on Tom, we have a chat and for once, we don't have a fight, leave his house feeling strange and disappointed, maybe deep down I must enjoy fighting him. I am a lucky boy to have them as friends, they have given me so much. My mother says I will remember those three for the rest of my life, as we are all growing up together. My mother was right, no matter where I or they end up I will always remember the days, nights, laughter, tears and madness I spent with these three, learning about new music, new clothes and even new points of view. But I am still a kid so that is a long way off. My mother was surprised when I said I am happy to be back at school, but she doesn't know I am planning a revolution and I want to bring Rydens down and it's new headmaster, my old year head, Chicken George.

The Rydens Revolution has grown from Rash, Stone, Curtis and me to about 20 or so nutty kids. Stone is clever and a good leader, he says we need to wait and find the right time, but he said we need to cause chaos whenever and wherever we can, which has become our motto "Chaos whenever and wherever", and it's written all over the walls at school, a sign that the revolution is coming. A few weeks in and lessons are in turmoil, classrooms vandalised. There is a feeling of unrest in the air, high tension, really intense. I thrive on being intense. Susie often gets annoyed with me for being so intense, I think it sometimes scares her, but I don't mean to, she says she feels it smothers her sometimes and I need to back off.

I was just about to start the afternoon lesson, after lunch break, double chemistry, CSE, full of all the nutters who don't learn fuck all, but love the lessons. For a laugh during lunch we wandered into the science block and tried to take off the door from C1, with the help of a few screwdrivers nicked from metal work this morning. Nearly got it off before we heard someone shout out for us to stop, so we legged it leaving the door half hanging off its hinges. At least we caused chaos, and that's what it is all about. However, all afternoon lessons have been cancelled, as Mr George Young, our new headmaster, otherwise known as Chicken George, has called an emergency assembly for all the 4th and 5th years.

This has never happened before, got a hunch our regime of "Chaos whenever and wherever" is getting to him, I am happy, very happy in fact. I suppose my hatred for teachers started in 1979 when Mrs Titchener wrongly accused me of trying to torture a horse, walked home that day hated by my fellow pupils, then I discovered The Jam. As you know, The Jam gave me hope, belief and a look, without them I may have gone under, believing the teachers who were telling me I was useless and a failure. From that fateful day my love for Mod has grown and my hatred for school has increased.

As I enter the hall I see Rash and make a point of sitting next to him, he's great at making stupid noises. I see Susie, Tina and the rest her friends sitting a couple of rows in front to my left. Susie mouths the words "what have you done?" I mouth the words "nothing" she smiles and shakes her head in a jokey way. The words of Fly by The Jam entered into my head, the first true love song I ever heard, and mouth to her "And look forward to see you, now I can't live without you", she blows me a kiss, I feel good and sit down. Rash puts his arm round me and says "he looks drunk" pointing at Chicken George.

Fuck me, he is right, Chicken George seems to be swaying, nearly falling back and then pulling himself up. Behind him is a huge, and I mean a huge, Union Jack. On his left are all the teachers, some of them you know, Mrs Vaughn, now the assistant head, ugly as ever. Miss Alderton, my history teacher, I am getting a bit of a crush on her, as she looks like a hippie, seen loads of photos of hippie girls in the sixties in America, I must admit they are gorgeous, try not to look at her too much as Susie might notice, as she knows I have a thing for her. The sadist PE Teacher Mr Hare is also here, heard he slept with a few of the girls, maybe rumours, not sure, but he does fancy himself, and a few more teachers who even bore me just talking about them, as I hate them so much.

Everyone settles down as Chicken George walks or should I say staggers towards the mic on the wooden stand, he coughs and clears his throat, whilst he is doing this, Rash gives me a dead leg. "I am no fool", says Chicken George.

"Says who? " shouts Paul Foyle, a rough boy. Mr Hare loving the moment, jumps down from the stage, marches up to Foyle, pulls him out and tries to march him out of the hall. A lot of our year get up, we are ready, we want war. Hare sees this and puts Foyle down, walks back to the stage rather sheepishly. Then Curtis the Cat shouts out "let the man speak", he's second in command or so he thinks, the kids obey.

Chicken George looks tense, I look over to my left where the 5th year sit, who are trying to give us dirty looks, I look back at my lot who are staring back. Chicken George starts speaking again "It's no secret that a small proportion of this school are behaving troublesomely and this will not be tolerated, today it stops. Discipline will be reinstated, rules will be obeyed."

I am smiling, Curtis is standing up putting his finger over his mouth telling no one to speak, like me he wants to see where Chicken George is going with this. "Great Britain was once a great country. It was the envy of the world, in fact it ruled the world, yes ruled the world. We had an Empire, an Empire where the sun never set, then we lost it, and we became an island, an island for British people, British people, yet we were safe and everyone knew their place, be it the chimney sweep or the prime minster, we were exultant and prosperous, but it was for British people, people born and bred in this country, not immigrants, but white Christian people." He pauses, our year sit in total disbelief, amusement and silence whilst some of the 5th year say a few 'hear hears'

"After the war, everything was good, the economy was growing again, living the British way of life, the best life a man could have. Then in the 50's we invited them over" he points straight at Rash, who like me, looks surprised and tickled, "Yes you look shocked, but having a job on the trains and the underground wasn't enough, or living in a rundown part of London, you fornicated and spawned little nig nogs, moved across Great Britain, bringing all the shit that came with your kind. Then, about ten years ago that wog Idi Amin dumped loads of Ugandan Asians here, the NHS opened their doors to pakis and darkies, I don't want my skin touched by your kind," he points at Mahen, an Indian kid who joined Rydens last year, good lad, likes a laugh and brilliant footballer. Mahen is in stitches, Chicken George's words can't hurt us, yet some of the 5th year all agree.

He carries on "I want Dr Jones not Dr Patel, I don't want curries, I want roast beef, I don't want pizzas" then he points at me "Wop food, garlic and more garlic, we won the war, Italy didn't."

I yawn and make sure he sees it, heard it all before, a few of the 5th year look in my direction with hatred in their eyes, I just give the V's up. Curtis is telling everyone to sit tight, whilst Stone is leaning forward fists clenched ready to go. Chicken George is working himself up into a frenzy.

"In 1968, I was in Birmingham, April it was, a meeting of the Conservative Party, the great Enoch Powell got up and gave this speech, stupidly called by the press the Rivers of Blood speech. It was a wonderful speech that foretold the terrible strife ahead with all the immigrants being allowed into Great Britain. I stood, listened and admired as a younger man than I am today, I was so enthralled and excited by it, that I got a full erection." The whole of my year burst out into laughter, even some the 5th year join in, whilst the teachers on the stage, apart from Mrs Vaughn, look stunned "Yes you may snigger, but it was the biggest, hardest and best erection I have ever had, the most proudest one I've ever had. I wish I could have taken a photo of it and framed it, I was so proud of my hard on that day."

Andrew Davies shouts out "Have another drink", as it is so clear that only a drunk man could address a room of school kids like this. George nods bends down and from behind the stand pulls out a huge bottle of scotch "Thank you, don't mind if I do" the teachers are now starting to pull away. "Did your wife like your cock that night" shouts out Tina, Susie starts laughing.

" No, no, no and no….that erection was too good for her. It was pure power, throbbing veins and a big hard helmet." Curtis looks round and gives the OK for us to start shouting "You must have fucked a chicken with it," shouts Lofty. Chicken George leans on the stand and collects his thoughts. "Chicken George, oh yes, only heard that since the bloody TV show about the coons being freed from slavery. No I have never fucked a chicken, a donkey yes, but that was a long, long time ago". "With a long, long cock….sir" George shakes his head and has another drink. "It's OK sir, tell us," shouts Mark Harris. Everyone, including teachers, are in total silence, this is brilliant. We have pushed him so much with "Chaos whenever and wherever" that mentally he couldn't take it, once we had shown we didn't care for his rule, he didn't know what to do, thought he'd just have a drink and confess all.

"It was the 50's, I was a young man away from home, working on farms in Somerset, saving up for... I can't remember what I was saving up for. I was alone yes, the Somerset girls were happy to eat my fish and chip suppers and drink the light ales I bought them, what did I get in return, heartache, real heartache. I'd wander off home after yet another night of rejection, drunk, and there was Ernie."

"Ernie who sir?"

"Ernie the donkey, so lovely, so kind, with a great back side."

I am starting to think that this has got to be a joke, if not, then why is a man who fucks animals, a sloppy drunk and who gets sexually excited by fascist rhetoric in charge of children, well, some might say that actually he probably has the right credentials. Then I realise all my life, well early part of my life I've been waiting to say this joke, so I jump up, "Are you the front end of an ass?"

"What?"

"Are you the front end of an ass?"

"No, I am not"

"What about the back end of an ass?"

"Shut up, no I am not"

Got him "So... you are no end of an ass."

The whole school roars with laughter, clearly Curtis the Cat knows the joke and says "fuck off you red nosed bastard." Shit I am like my father, but the other way, totally obsessed and inspired by clowns, I love madcap humour, what is wrong with me. "The bloody wop" George screams.

"Yes I know sir, who won the war" says Rash in my defence.

"Oh, the gollywog speaks, well if it hadn't been for William Wilberforce, you lot would still be in chains."

Now some of the 5th years cheer. They don't care that he fucks animals, now I have had enough, I nod at Curtis the Cat, he nods back, makes eyes for him to get Stone's attention, Stone looks at me I mouth the words - "Kill the fascist."

Stone looks at me puzzled. I mouth the words again, he looks at me as if to say he doesn't understand, so I pull out my jotter pad, write them down in big letters with my biro and show them to him. Stones' eyes light up, he nods and gets up, if he leads the charge the others will follow. Some of the 5th year get up to see Stone running towards the stage, George seems to run back, in fact he does, he dashes behind the curtains only to appear seconds later holding a sword, a fucking sword.

"Stupid boy, don't think I've not come prepared," the whole school stands up, whilst the teachers, including Mrs Vaughn, start to leave the stage. Stone stops in his tracks, then a cricket bat flies through the air. Stone catches it with such style, grabs it like a light sabre, always thought he might be a Jedi, he jumps on stage facing the fascist. Chicken George goes for the Errol Flynn pose in one of those swashbuckling black and white films, and shouts out "en –guard."

He moves his body sideways and lurches forward with a sword in his right hand and his left arm behind his back, and bends his knees slightly, I think he's done this before. Stone steps back and swings his cricket bat just like Obi-Wan Kenobi, it certainly is good vs evil.

Chicken George swings with the sword, Stone is good as he pulls the bat to block the attack. The sword is slightly wedged into the wood of the bat, Stone uses this advantage and pulls Chicken George, or should I say Donkey George, towards him, as he does he head butts our crazy and drunk, headmaster, George wobbles, manages to pull the sword free. As he pulls it out, Stone is shaken and George lunges out with a kick to the stomach.

By the way I am still in total disbelief at what I am witnessing but also loving every second, this is every school boy's dream. The kick to the gut undoes Stone as he hits the stage, some of the new 5th year cheer, fucking wankers, this man has admitted to fucking donkeys, fucking an animal, yet you support him. I look to Curtis the Cat, he is snarling, ready for action, he catches my eye I point to the 5th Years and simply say "Take them."

Told you I was really the leader and I don't need to repeat it once, he nods and shouts out "4th year all the fighters come here, we are united, we are strong." I am actually thrilled by Curtis the Cat's command, he's like Vinnie, he understands warfare and conflict and the deliverance of those words are as brilliant as Paul Weller screaming Eton Rifles live. I feel the power in the room, kids from different backgrounds, religions and even colour uniting against our deranged headmaster and his followers.

The girls and boys that aren't into fighting start to rush to the back for the hall's exit, the fighters and the ones that think they are, run towards Curtis the Cat, who is standing on a chair giving out orders. I must admit I am no fighter, hidden behind Vinnie, Snowy and other Mods, but I have to join in, firstly I helped to create this and these rough boys are my friends, these kids make me laugh at school every day. But before I can go on a rampage I need to find my sunshine girl, the girl whose love gives me light in my dark and twisted mind, who believes in me, why, I don't know, she must see something in me which I can't, but maybe I will, maybe I will. I see her with Tina, she doesn't seem scared... in fact she seems to be thriving on all this madness, our eyes meet and we smile, like we always do. I walk forward amongst the rushing crowd, no one knocks into me, I sway and move, Susie raises her eyebrows to say she's impressed, I hold out my hand and she puts hers forward so I can pull her towards me, whilst all around the fights are breaking out.

I briefly look at the stage and see Stone now swinging from the curtains smacking the cricket bat down hard on Chicken George, who seems to be wavering. Stone is strong, all the other teachers have left the stage and seem too frightened to walk, apart from Miss Alderton. She is heading towards the entrance, no one dares go for her, everyone likes her, boys and girls, why? 'cos she talks to us with respect and about the things we like, she doesn't dismiss it or put it down, thinking school is better. I remember her seeing me reading an interview with Paul Weller in the NME just before history, she didn't confiscate the paper, just asked to borrow it, she gave it back to me the next day, saying she can understand why

I like The Jam and I should meet her nephew as he is nuts about them, I know the feeling.

As Miss Alderton walks past she smiles and says - "best school riot I've ever seen… enjoy." I laugh, really laugh. Why can't all teachers be like her, get to know us, don't order us about 'cos you're the adult, get to like us, be our friend, not our enemy, sure you'd see more kids enjoying school. All these rules and regulations rammed down our throat. Look at that bastard who's our headmaster, a drunk, a donkey shagger and a rabid racist, you tell me, is he better than me, is he? Is he fuck.

I pull Susie towards me, kiss her cute nose and say "Get out of here luv, it's going to explode, there will be punishment, some of us may even be expelled, or sent to prison. I can't leave, you are my girlfriend and these are my friends in time of war." Susie fixes her eyes upon me, kisses me on the mouth "Kill them baby", she turns me round so I am facing the entrance, she slowly pulls away letting go of my hand, gives me a kiss and says "the moment I saw you lost but beautiful in your new suit at Crutchfield Lane, I just wanted to be your girlfriend, I just wanted to, it felt right."

I can't reply, I am so touched and this is crazy, a riot going on all round me and the love of my life declaring her feelings amongst it all, madness total madness. She walks slowly back, turns round and walks towards the entrance, I can't take my eyes off her, just like an angel she leaves the hall. My mouth is dry and my stomach is full of butterflies, is this love? I don't know, I really don't know, then my Romeo moment is broken as a body crashes into me.

It's Paul Adams from the year above, covered in blood and George Butler is throwing punches. Everywhere is a running battle, Curtis the Cat shouting orders, a group of my year are surrounding the other teachers, they look petrified even Mr Hare. It does cross my mind to execute them, one by one, behead them, but they ain't worth a prison sentence. My adrenaline is going, this is such an amazing experience.

I look at the stage, Stone has got Chicken George in a headlock and rubbing his knuckles in his head, Stone looks up and smiles, like the nutter he is, but he's my nutter, he's my mate, he's a Punk and I am a Mod, yet we are mates, doesn't really matter what tribe you belong to, in all honesty, no, it doesn't. I notice the large windows in the hall are still intact, not one smashed, my God how long I have yearned for this. Then Tom Brendan, a soul boy from the 5th year takes a swing at me, I duck, I can see it coming, from behind Rash smacks him on the back of his head with a chair. Brendan doesn't go down but stumbles so I kick him in the stomach hard, then he goes down.

I put my hands in front of my face and wave to Rash to pass me the chair, which he does. I take it with both hands, as well as saying thanks - doesn't cost to be polite. I walk with pace towards the large window, raise the chair above my head with the metal legs pointing forward. I aim for the middle, fire and bang the whole of the window smashes, glass flies everywhere, people cover their faces, I have wanted to do this for such a long time. The smashing of the window brings the fighting to an end, everyone just stops.

I wish Vinnie was here, he would have loved it, this has his name all over it. I look round… the school is in ruins, a smashed up assembly hall, scared teachers, a half dead headmaster, kids with cuts and bruises and ruined school uniforms. I have to say, today is the best day I have ever had at school. In the distance I hear the police sirens, PC Macdonald and his mates will come in wielding their truncheons. But we will be ready, we will fight back. For too long we have been quiet, I am not just talking about Mods but us, kids, teenagers, young adults as the bloody BBC calls us, told to 'do this', 'wear this', 'don't go there', today we are united, we will fight.

The other week or so Norway beat England for a World Cup qualifier. Sportsnight played a clip of the Norwegian commenter going mad, I think it went like this "Lord Nelson, Lord Beaverbrook, Sir Winston Churchill, Sir Anthony Eden, Clement Attlee, Henry Cooper, Lady Diana, we have beaten them all, we have beaten them all. Maggie Thatcher, can you hear me? Maggie Thatcher your boys took a hell of a beating! Your boys took a hell of a beating!" Loved it, so did my parents and my brother. I stand looking up at the ceiling, arms wide open and shout "Can you hear me Thatcher? Maggie Thatcher, can you hear me?, you've got a fucked up generation coming through, fucked up by your principles, not ours, we will fight you, we will stop you, we are young, beautiful, energetic and dangerous." This is met by loud cheers, mainly from my year, in fact I get a standing ovation. I feel like Peter O'Toole in Lawrence of Arabia when he walks on a train's roof that has been ambushed.

Then my year start shouting "Who the fuck is Maggie Thatcher" over and over, it's beautiful and endearing chaos. I have dreamt of a revolution since Middle School. I am caught in the moment, I love being young, I love being a Mod, it has opened my mind and eyes to so much, so much more than school, church or work will ever do. Gave me a purpose, a dress code, friends, a journey into music, adventure, an identity, fun, a girlfriend and the courage to be creative. Paul Weller, Ian Page, Pete Townsend, Steve Marriott, Reggie King, Otis Redding, Wilson Pickett, so many of you, take a bow. I feel a tap on my shoulder, it's Rash, he's holding a packet of Rothmans I take one and light up, inhale and blow the smoke out, thinking isn't life really just about having a crafty cigarette.

The End

 **Matteo Sedazzari,** like the hero of Crafty Cigarette, became a Jam fan by accident after playing All Mod Cons during the school Easter holiday, a moment when, like many of his generation, Buckler, Foxton and Weller changed his life forever. He loved the music so much that he more or less became a Mod overnight. Inspired by the philosophy of The Jam, and unable to emulate them in music, he turned to writing, producing a fanzine entitled Positive Energy of Madness during the height of Acid House which, in fact, did feature the first ever interview with Weller after the disbandment of The Style Council. Positive Energy of Madness dissolved as a fanzine in 1994 and resurfaced in 2003 as an online magazine, don't ask what he was doing during those years, he doesn't know himself. Building a following, Matteo Sedazzari wanted to say goodbye to the past, think forward, just like a true Mod, Positive Energy of Madness was ditched and replaced by ZANI, a quirky and more modern site, which has attracted interviews with Bobby Womack, Clem Burke of Blondie, Alan McGee, Chas Smash of Madness, Shaun Ryder of Black Grape/Happy Mondays and many more. Inspired by writers Hunter S Thompson, Harlan Ellison, Mark Twain, Iceberg Slim, Patricia Highsmith, Daphne du Maurier and films like The Loneliness of the Long Distance Runner, Saturday Night and Sunday Morning, Z, Babylon, Midnight Cowboy and many more.

Matteo Sedazzari resides in Surrey, outside of writing, supports Juventus, travels to Italy and Spain, likes to dress well and being happy.

ZANI is an independent online magazine for readers interested in contemporary culture, covering Music, Film & TV, Sport, Art amongst other cultural topics. Relevant to modern times ZANI is a dynamic website and a flagship for creative movement and thinking wherever our readers live in the world.

Please look at ZANI here www.zani.co.uk

Or like or follow us here.
www.facebook/zanionline
www.twitter.com/ZANIEzine

19935473R00092

Printed in Great Britain
by Amazon